Early Praise for *Effective Go Recipes*

I have known Miki for years, and he is one of the very few authors that have material I can trust without question. Miki takes the time to research each topic and finds the right people to review the content to guarantee the material is accurate and practical. Miki's experience working on development teams and products is what sets his material apart from many other authors who tend to write books with only a cursory knowledge of engineering principles. If you are looking for real, practical development training from an experienced software developer, Miki is your guy.

➤ **Bill Kennedy**
    Managing Partner, Ardan Labs

It's such a refreshing change to see a highly technical book that brings a human element alongside technical excellence. It really does feel like Miki is speaking and teaching you, personally. I need to congratulate Miki and his editors for bringing such a personal tone on the page.

➤ **Adelina Simion**
    Education Engineer, Spectro Cloud

As a senior engineer with experience in both open source and proprietary software, I've tackled numerous challenges in building and maintaining projects. *Effective Go Recipes: Fast Solutions to Common Tasks* is an invaluable resource that distills the collective wisdom of the Go community. While Go may appear simple, it's enriched with patterns and practices that have evolved over time. This book is a concise guide to these patterns, offering a ready reference for both budding and seasoned Go developers. I firmly believe every Go enthusiast and any organization utilizing Go should have a copy on their shelf.

➤ **Yoni Davidson**
  Core Engineer, Tabnine

I have worked with Go for almost a decade on open source and closed source projects.

Finding some well-written common practice for those projects, and especially around ramping up junior engineers, was always a challenge. I have found *Effective Go Recipes: Fast Solutions to Common Tasks* to be a Swiss Army knife for such recipes. A very clear and down-to-earth guide on how to construct your own Go program.

I would recommend it to everyone who writes production Go code.

➤ **Aviv Laufer**
  Senior Principal Software Engineer, Rokt

Effective Go Recipes

Fast Solutions to Common Tasks

Miki Tebeka

The Pragmatic Bookshelf

Dallas, Texas

When we are aware that a term used in this book is claimed as a trademark, the designation is printed with an initial capital letter or in all capitals.

The Pragmatic Starter Kit, The Pragmatic Programmer, Pragmatic Programming, Pragmatic Bookshelf, PragProg and the linking *g* device are trademarks of The Pragmatic Programmers, LLC.

Every precaution was taken in the preparation of this book. However, the publisher assumes no responsibility for errors or omissions, or for damages that may result from the use of information (including program listings) contained herein.

For our complete catalog of hands-on, practical, and Pragmatic content for software developers, please visit *https://pragprog.com*.

The team that produced this book includes:

Publisher:	Dave Thomas
COO:	Janet Furlow
Executive Editor:	Susannah Davidson
Development Editor:	Margaret Eldridge
Copy Editor:	L. Sakhi MacMillan
Indexing:	Potomac Indexing, LLC
Layout:	Gilson Graphics

For sales, volume licensing, and support, please contact *support@pragprog.com*.

For international rights, please contact *rights@pragprog.com*.

ISBN-13: 978-1-68050-846-8
Book version: P1.0—April 2024

Contents

Preface

Cooking with Go

Go is a simple language. The Go 1.20 language specification[1] is about 105 pages; in contrast, the Java 20 language specification[2] comes to 854 pages. But even though Go is simple, it doesn't mean you can't do a lot with it.

As any TV chef will repeatedly tell you, you can make amazing dishes with a few basic, simple ingredients. The same goes for software—you can build sleek, fast, and useful applications using a simple language like Go.

A good way to learn to cook is by following recipes. These recipes might be from professionals or handed down from generation to generation. At the beginning, you'll follow recipes to the letter. But once you get more experience, you'll start to diverge and add your own touch.

The same goes for programming recipes. If you're a novice, you'll probably want to follow the recipes almost to the letter. But once you gain experience, you'll develop your own way of doing things. Hopefully, once at the expert level, you'll share your own recipes.

Who Are You?

This book is written for Go developers (doh!). The recipes in this book vary in difficulty. Some recipes will be a good fit for a Go beginner, while others will help more advanced developers.

This book won't teach you Go—you'll find many good books, tutorials, and courses out there for that (I teach some of them). To use this book, you should also be familiar with working in the terminal and know some client-server terms and technologies, such as HTTP and sockets.

---

1. https://go.dev/ref/spec
2. https://docs.oracle.com/javase/specs/jls/se20/jls20.pdf

Reading This Book

This book is a collection of recipes. For each recipe, I tried to set the stage for when it is applicable, provide some context, light some candles ... (strike the last one, it's not that kind of book).

The recipes are split into sections, but there is overlap—you can talk about errors without knowing about interfaces. In each section, the recipes are sorted according to their difficulty level. Feel free to roam around; what I think as difficult might be easy for you.

A Foolish Consistency Is the Hobgoblin of Little Minds

We use some conventions in this book.

Code samples and terminal sessions look like this:

```
fmt.Println("Hello Gophers ♡")
```

Modern terminals are much wider than the common page width. In some cases I had to truncate output using ... or break long lines using \. For example:

```
$ go test -run NONE -fuzz . -fuzztime 10s
fuzz: elapsed: 0s, gathering baseline coverage: 0/2 completed
fuzz: elapsed: 0s, gathering baseline coverage: 2/2 completed, \
    now fuzzing with 12 workers
...
```

The code and examples show output from Go version 1.20. Some of the output might change in the future, but Go has a compatibility promise—things shouldn't change that much.

Wait! There's More! (online)

At the book's website[3] you can find the full source code used in this book. You'll also find a link to the errata page—please help your fellow readers and report any issues you find. And finally, you'll find a link to a discussion forum about the book.

Let's get cooking!

---

3. https://pragprog.com/titles/mtgo

Reading and Writing (I/O)

Your program communicates with the world using input and output (I/O for short). Go provides a great abstraction over I/O with the io.Reader and io.Writer interfaces. These interfaces are implemented by files, sockets, HTTP response bodies, and more.

While io.Reader and io.Writer give a standard API to I/O, there are many implementation-specific details you need to consider when working with I/O. In this chapter we'll look at in-memory I/O, compression, and memory mapped files for faster searching. We'll also see how you can implement these interfaces in your types and why you should do so.

Since files are a big part of I/O, we'll look at file paths (for example, /var/log/httpd.log) and how to manipulate them.

Recipe 1

Using In-Memory Readers and Writers to Support []byte

Task

You're working on the back end for a ride-sharing site. The back end is composed of several processes that communicate with each other. The existing implementation has code to serialize data, but it works with io.Reader and io.Writer. You want to explore shared memory as a medium to exchange data, and in shared memory you need to work with []byte.

Solution

You start by looking at the current code. You see a Ride struct:

io/marshal/marshal.go
```go
// Ride is a ride record.
type Ride struct {
    ID       int
    Time     time.Time
    Duration time.Duration
    Distance float64
    Price    float64
}
```

Then you look at the current NewDecoder, which returns a *Decoder:

io/marshal/marshal.go
```go
// NewDecoder returns a new Decoder.
func NewDecoder(r io.Reader) *Decoder {
    return &Decoder{json.NewDecoder(r)}
}
```

What you need to do is to convert a []byte to an io.Reader. This is where bytes.NewReader comes in handy:

io/marshal/marshal.go
```go
// UnmarshalRide returns a Ride from serialized data.
func UnmarshalRide(data []byte, ride *Ride) error {
    r := bytes.NewReader(data)
    return NewDecoder(r).DecodeRide(ride)
}
```

Discussion

bytes.NewReader and its cousins strings.NewReader, bytes.Buffer, and others create in-memory io.Reader and io.Writer around concrete types. They're helpful when dealing with APIs that only work with io.Reader (such as encoding/gob).

I use these in-memory readers and writers a lot while testing. I start with a file with a list of concrete examples, then read each case and pass it, wrapped in an in-memory reader, to a decoder and test it. To learn more about testing, head over to Chapter 13, Testing Your Code, on page 193, and to learn more about memory mapped files, see Recipe 7, Searching in a Memory Mapped File, on page 16.

Recipe 2

Compressing Old Log Files

Task

You're "on loan" to the operations team—you're going to help them by writing some utilities. The operations team lead sends you the following email:

> Welcome to the team!
>
> Your first task, should you choose to accept it, is to write a "janitor" utility. This utility should go over a given directory and compress any log file (having .log suffix) that is over a month old. After compressing, you should compare the content of the compressed file with the original file (say, using SHA1) and if it matches, delete the original file.
>
> This message won't destruct in five seconds.

After some back-and-forth, you agree that "a month" equals thirty days and that you'll use gzip compression.

Shell Magic

 I know you can complete this task with a combination of the Unix find and gzip utilities. However, the goal here is to learn how to work with files and not to practice Unix command-line tricks.

Solution

You write a gzCompress function that gets a source file and compresses it using gzip to the destination file:

```
files/janitor/janitor.go
Line 1  // gzCompress compresses src to dest with gzip compression.
     -  func gzCompress(src, dest string) error {
     -      file, err := os.Open(src)
     -      if err != nil {
     5          return err
     -      }
     -      defer file.Close()
     -
     -      out, err := os.Create(dest)
    10      if err != nil {
     -          return err
     -      }
```

```
         defer out.Close()

15       w := gzip.NewWriter(out)
         defer w.Close()

         // Update metadata, must be before io.Copy
         w.Name = src
20       info, err := file.Stat()
         if err == nil {
             w.ModTime = info.ModTime()
         }

25       if _, err := io.Copy(w, file); err != nil {
             os.Remove(dest)
             return err
         }

30       return nil
     }
```

Then you write shouldCompress, which checks if a file is older than a given time span:

files/janitor/janitor.go
```
func shouldCompress(path string, maxAge time.Duration) bool {
    info, err := os.Stat(path)
    if err != nil {
        log.Printf("warning: %q: can't get info: %s", path, err)
        return false
    }

    if info.IsDir() {
        return false
    }

    return time.Since(info.ModTime()) >= maxAge
}
```

And then you write filesToCompress, which will return a list of files that are older than a given time span in a directory:

files/janitor/janitor.go
```
func filesToCompress(dir string, maxAge time.Duration) ([]string, error) {
    root := os.DirFS(dir)
    logFiles, err := fs.Glob(root, "*.log")
    if err != nil {
        return nil, err
    }
```

```go
    var names []string
    for _, src := range logFiles {
        name := path.Join(dir, src)
        if shouldCompress(name, maxAge) {
            names = append(names, name)
        }
    }

    return names, nil
}
```

Then, to check that a file was compressed without issues, you write code to compare the file SHA1 signature:

```go
func fileSHA1(fileName string) (string, error) {
    file, err := os.Open(fileName)
    if err != nil {
        return "", nil
    }
    defer file.Close()

    var r io.Reader = file
    if path.Ext(fileName) == ".gz" {
        var err error
        r, err = gzip.NewReader(r)
        if err != nil {
            return "", err
        }
    }

    w := sha1.New()
    if _, err := io.Copy(w, r); err != nil {
        return "", err
    }

    sig := fmt.Sprintf("%x", w.Sum(nil))
    return sig, nil
}
func sameSig(file1, file2 string) (bool, error) {
    sig1, err := fileSHA1(file1)
    if err != nil {
        return false, err
    }

    sig2, err := fileSHA1(file2)
    if err != nil {
        return false, err
    }

    return sig1 == sig2, nil
}
```

Finally, you write compressFiles, which will compress only files older than the time span:

files/janitor/janitor.go

```go
func compressFiles(rootDir string, maxAge time.Duration) error {
    files, err := filesToCompress(rootDir, maxAge)
    if err != nil {
        return err
    }

    for _, src := range files {
        dest := src + ".gz"
        if err := gzCompress(src, dest); err != nil {
            return fmt.Errorf("%q: %w", src, err)
        }

        match, err := sameSig(src, dest)
        if err != nil {
            return err
        }

        if !match {
            return fmt.Errorf("%q <-> %q: signature don't match", src, dest)
        }

        if err := os.Remove(src); err != nil {
            log.Printf("warning: %q: can't delete - %s", src, err)
        }
    }

    return nil
}
```

Discussion

Reading is by far the most common operation you'll do with files. os.Open is a convenient, short way to open a file for reading.

On line 7, you use defer to make sure the file is closed. The operating system defines a limit on the number of open files a process can hold. On Unix systems, you can use the ulimit utility to see this limit.

On line 15, you wrap the output file with gzip.NewWriter. gzip.NewWriter also implements io.Writer, meaning it can be used by io.Copy.

*os.File implements many of the interfaces defined in the io package—io.Reader, io.Writer, and io.Closer—and you can pass it to any function accepting one of these interfaces.

On line 2, you use the os.Stat function to get information about the file.

You can do a lot of system-level work using functions from the os and io—read the docs and get familiar with these functions.

Recipe 3

Using bytes.Buffer to Generate SQL

Task

The ride-sharing application you're working on stores its data in a SQL database. The company wants to allow access to its data from an API.

You don't want to allow users to pass arbitrary SQL statements—it's a security risk (SQL injection), and it ties the database design to the API design.

First, you need to provide a function that, given a table name and a list of columns, returns a SQL query that will select this data from the database. For a table name rides and the columns id, time, and duration, you generate the following output:

```
SELECT
    id,
    time,
    duration
FROM rides;
```

Solution

You write a genSelect function that accepts a table name and a slice of columns and returns SQL as a string:

io/sql/sql.go
```
func genSelect(table string, columns []string) (string, error) {
    var buf bytes.Buffer

    if len(columns) == 0 {
        return "", fmt.Errorf("empty select")
    }

    fmt.Fprintln(&buf, "SELECT")
    for i, col := range columns {
        suffix := ","
        if i == len(columns)-1 {
            suffix = "" // No trailing comma in SQL
        }
```

```
        fmt.Fprintf(&buf, "      %s%s\n", col, suffix)
    }
    fmt.Fprintf(&buf, "FROM %s;", table)
    return buf.String(), nil
}
```

Discussion

genSelect uses bytes.Buffer as an io.Writer interface. This way, the fmt function emits data into the buffer and not to the standard output. At the end of the function, you use the String method to return the accumulated string.

Using bytes.Buffer as in-memory io.Writer gives us two advantages:

- It simplifies our code generation algorithm
- It allows us to use the fmt package

You'd be surprised how many times using an algorithm that generates data on the fly, such as printing, will make your code simpler. By using an in-memory io.Writer, we're able to emit data as it comes and not accumulate it and then return it.

For fancier code or text generation, check out the text/template and html/template built-in packages.

Recipe 4

Conditionally Decompressing Files

Task

You recently changed the layout of your company's website. To be backward compatible, you emit an HTTP redirect status code to tell clients accessing the old pages where to find the new location.

After a while, you want to check how many clients are still trying to access the old pages. If nobody is accessing the old pages, you can delete some legacy code.

The HTTP server log files are saved to the logs directory, and some of them are compressed. Let's see what's there:

```
$ ls logs
http-1.log.gz  http-3.log.gz  http-5.log.gz  http-7.log
http-2.log.gz  http-4.log.gz  http-6.log.gz  http-8.log
```

You see that all log files, except 7 and 8, are compressed with gzip compression.

Solution

You start by writing a numRedirects function that gets an io.Reader and returns the total number of lines and the number of lines that have an HTTP redirect directive:

io/redirects/redirects.go
```
// numRedirects returns the total number of lines and the number of lines
// with an HTTP redirect
func numRedirects(r io.Reader) (int, int, error) {
    s := bufio.NewScanner(r)
    nLines, nRedirects := 0, 0
    for s.Scan() {
        nLines++
        // Example:
        // 203.252.212.44 - - [01/Aug/1995:03:45:47 -0400] \
        // "GET /ksc.html HTTP/1.0" 200 7280
        fields := strings.Fields(s.Text())
        code := fields[len(fields)-2] // code is one before last
        if code[0] == '3' {             // HTTP redirect is 3XX
            nRedirects++
        }
    }
    if err := s.Err(); err != nil {
        return -1, -1, err
    }
    return nLines, nRedirects, nil
}
```

Once numRedirects is written, we can get to work. First find out what log files are in the logs directory:

io/redirects/redirects.go
```
matches, err := filepath.Glob("logs/http-*.log*")
if err != nil {
    log.Fatalf("error: %s", err)
}
```

Then iterate over the files and open them one by one for reading:

io/redirects/redirects.go
```
nLines, nRedirects := 0, 0
for _, fileName := range matches {
    file, err := os.Open(fileName)
    if err != nil {
        log.Fatalf("error: %s", err)
    }
```

Here you can use io.Reader. os.Open returns a *os.File, which implements io.Reader. If the file name ends with .gz, we can wrap this reader with a gzip.Reader. In both cases, compressed and not compressed, we pass an io.Reader to the numRedirects function:

io/redirects/redirects.go
```
Line 1  var r io.Reader = file
   -    if strings.HasSuffix(fileName, ".gz") {
   -        r, err = gzip.NewReader(r)
   -        if err != nil {
   5            log.Fatalf("%q - %v", fileName, err)
   -        }
   -    }
   -
   -    nl, nr, err := numRedirects(r)
  10    if err != nil {
   -        log.Fatalf("%q - %v", fileName, err)
   -    }
   -    nLines += nl
   -    nRedirects += nr
```

Finally, we can print the result:

io/redirects/redirects.go
```
fmt.Printf("%d redirects in %d lines\n", nRedirects, nLines)
```

The result prints this:

```
627 redirects in 8000 lines
```

About 7.8% of the requests still use the old structure. Sadly, you still need to keep your legacy code around and maybe reach out to customers and ask them to change their code.

Discussion

By designing numRedirects to get an io.Reader as parameter, you make it more flexible. numRedirects doesn't care if the input comes from a compressed file or not.

The numRedirects function is oblivious to *how* we created the reader—it can be a file, a compressed file, a socket, or anything else that implements io.Reader.

Every time you work with byte-oriented input or output, consider using io.Reader and io.Writer. It'll simplify your code and make your function more flexible than using concrete types such as *os.File or net.Conn.

Note that in line 3 we use = (equal) and not :=. If you use :=, then the r inside the if statement will be a new variable, and the function level r won't be affected. The := is a handy shortcut, but you should use it with care.

Recipe 5

Implementing io.Writer for Frequency Calculation

Task

You're working at a fraud detection company, and they want to check if companies are "cooking" the books. Your initial task is to use Benford's law,[1] which checks the distribution of leading digits in numbers.

Solution

You decide to write a struct that will implement io.Writer and count leading digits. This way you can use io.Copy and process data coming from anything implementing io.Reader, such as files, sockets, and more.

Here's the struct definition:

io/wtr/wtr.go
```go
// DigitsFreq calculates leading digit frequency.
type DigitsFreq struct {
    Freqs map[rune]int // Leading digit frequency

    inNum bool // local state
}
```

Now you can implement io.Writer. You get a []byte and update the leading digits distribution:

---

1. https://mathworld.wolfram.com/BenfordsLaw.html

io/wtr/wtr.go

```
Line 1  // Write implements io.Writer.
   -    func (d *DigitsFreq) Write(data []byte) (int, error) {
   -        if d.Freqs == nil {
   -            d.Freqs = make(map[rune]int)
   5        }

   -        for _, b := range data {
   -            if r := rune(b); unicode.IsDigit(r) {
   -                if !d.inNum { // it's a leading digit
  10                    d.Freqs[r]++
   -                    d.inNum = true
   -                }
   -                continue
   -            }
  15
   -            // Here it's not a digit
   -            if d.inNum {
   -                d.inNum = false
   -            }
  20        }

   -        return len(data), nil
   -    }
```

That's it! Here's some testing code to check:

io/wtr/wtr.go

```
Line 1      data := `
   -    We have 1234
   -    then 2342
   -    then 110
   5    then 37
   -    `

   -        var df DigitsFreq
   -        io.Copy(&df, strings.NewReader(data))
   -        for r, c := range df.Freqs {
  10            fmt.Printf("%c → %d\n", r, c)
   -        }
```

The preceding code prints the following:

```
1 → 2
2 → 1
3 → 1
```

Discussion

By having your type implement io.Reader or io.Writer, you can utilize a lot of the existing code in the standard library. Users of your code will also thank you since they don't need to learn a new way to work with your code.

You can see this approach in the standard library. For example, all digital hashing types in the crypto package (such as sha1) implement io.Writer.

You should also try to make your types valuable without an explicit New function. In line 3, we create the Freqs map inside the Write method so in line 7 we can declare a variable of this type without initializing any fields. This idiom is sometimes called "Make the zero value useful" (attributed to Rob Pike[2]).

Recipe 6

Using os.Pipe for Dynamic Data Generation

Task

You're working on a back end for a ride-hailing company. Jose, your co-worker, writes a code that dynamically queries the database on rides at a given location. The code will execute a query and then start a new goroutine that will generate the data. Finally, the code returns a channel you can receive from.

You need to use this code in an HTTP handler that accepts a query and encodes the data in JSON format.

Solution

Let's first look at the existing code. Here is the Ride struct:

```
io/pipe/pipe.go
// Ride is an information on a ride.
type Ride struct {
    Time     time.Time
    Distance float64
    Price    float64
}
```

And here's the Query method signature:

---

2.   https://go-proverbs.github.io/

```
io/pipe/pipe.go
// QueryRidesIn returns a channel of Rides location.
// It'll close it once there's no more data.
func (c *Conn) QueryRidesIn(location string) <-chan Ride {
```

Instead of writing everything in the HTTP handler, you start by writing an encodeRides function that reads from a channel and encodes to an io.WriteCloser:

```
io/pipe/pipe.go
// encodeRides encodes rides from ch into w
func encodeRides(ch <-chan Ride, w io.WriteCloser) error {
    enc := json.NewEncoder(w)
    defer w.Close() // Signal no-more-data on function exit

    for r := range ch {
        if err := enc.Encode(r); err != nil {
            return err
        }
    }

    return nil
}
```

This code is small, self-contained, and easy to test even without an HTTP handler.

Now we use encodeRides in our HTTP handler. The handler has the usual HTTP handler function signature:

```
io/pipe/pipe.go
func queryHandler(w http.ResponseWriter, r *http.Request) {
```

You start by reading the location query from the HTTP request body:

```
io/pipe/pipe.go
data, err := io.ReadAll(io.LimitReader(r.Body, maxSize))
if err != nil {
    http.Error(w, "can't read body", http.StatusBadRequest)
    return
}
location := string(data)
```

Then connect to the database and execute a query, getting a channel in return:

```
io/pipe/pipe.go
conn, err := Dial(dbDSN)
if err != nil {
    http.Error(w, "can't connect", http.StatusInternalServerError)
    return
}
ch := conn.QueryRidesIn(location)
```

Now you use os.Pipe to create an io.Reader and io.Writer:

io/pipe/pipe.go
```
rp, wp, err := os.Pipe()
if err != nil {
    http.Error(w, "can't create pipe", http.StatusInternalServerError)
    return
}
```

What's left is simple—start a goroutine to encode the data with the writer side, and use io.Copy to copy the encoded data to the response:

io/pipe/pipe.go
```
go encodeRides(ch, wp)
_, err = io.Copy(w, rp)
if err != nil {
    // Can't send error to client here
    log.Printf("error: can't encode: %s", err)
}
```

Discussion

Pipes are one of the basics of Unix philosophy. In the command line, you can use pipes to connect the output of one program to the input of another.

Knuth vs. McIlroy

From the early days of computing comes this great story: to illustrate Literate Programming, Knuth wrote a wonderful, ten-plus-page program to read a file of text, determine the n most frequently used words, and print out a sorted list of those words along with their frequencies.

Reading this, McIlroy wrote a six-command shell pipe that did exactly the same thing:

```
tr -cs A-Za-z '\n' |
tr A-Z a-z |
sort |
uniq -c |
sort -rn |
sed ${1}q
```

Unix pipelines *are* powerful—learn to use them.

The os.Pipe command is efficient. It will use the underlying Unix pipe mechanism and won't consume too much memory. Make sure to close the write side of the pipe when there's no more data, otherwise the read side will hang.

The data generated is one JSON object per line. Here's an example:

```
{"Time":"2023-06-29T18:02:49.043508995+03:00","Distance":7.10,"Price":16.52}
{"Time":"2023-06-29T18:02:50.044614641+03:00","Distance":1.45,"Price":22.61}
{"Time":"2023-06-29T18:02:51.044914461+03:00","Distance":4.39,"Price":5.45}
{"Time":"2023-06-29T18:02:52.045205143+03:00","Distance":10.1,"Price":32.64}
{"Time":"2023-06-29T18:02:53.045507559+03:00","Distance":7.17,"Price":8.25}
{"Time":"2023-06-29T18:02:54.045809023+03:00","Distance":7.10,"Price":32.33}
{"Time":"2023-06-29T18:02:55.046118428+03:00","Distance":8.16,"Price":20.24}
```

As a whole, this is not valid JSON—it's known as "JSON lines" format. The Go encoding/json.Decoder can handle this output, but other clients might not. (See also *Streaming POST Requests*.)

Recipe 7

Searching in a Memory Mapped File

Task

Your company is ingesting data from several sources. To make it easier for customers, you allow them to send data in any format they want. Your job is to parse all the various formats and load them into the company database.

One client decided to send data in a very *interesting* format. The format has binary, text, and JSON all mingled together. You need to extract the location information from these files.

Here's a part of the file:

```
files/mmap/data.txt
dummy text #0
dummy text #1
dummy text #2
dummy text #3
dummy text #4
dummy text #5
1i6v2q-,*M7!^:[Hc59TxswNhre}Rloc:{
    "lat": 32.519585,
    "lng": 35.015021
}NJ*o,B;n%{Z
'PaSL`Op)60~c"I1].MX[@\_=ik$xq/8(:4j5uTRt#3b-srwW+mv
dummy text #0
dummy text #1
```

You can see there's JSON location information that's prefixed with loc:. Since the data file can be big, you can't read it whole into memory. Reading one line or one chunk of the file will make the code complex.

Solution

You head over to Joe, who's been around forever and has seen things. After you describe the problem, he asks, "What about memory mapped files (mmap)?"

After reading some about mmap, you decide that Joe was right (again).

Using mmap on the data file will return a []byte that reflects the content of the file.

mmap is operating-system specific and is located at golang.org/x/sys/unix external package.

You start by defining a Location struct, which will be filled by the JSON parser:

files/mmap/locs.go
```go
// Location is location on Earth.
type Location struct {
    Lat float64
    Lng float64
}
```

Next, you open the file as usual with os.Open:

files/mmap/locs.go
```go
file, err := os.Open("data.txt")
if err != nil {
    log.Fatalf("error: %s", err)
}
defer file.Close()
```

And now, you use unix.Mmap to map the file into a []byte:

files/mmap/locs.go
```go
fi, err := file.Stat()
if err != nil {
    log.Fatalf("error: %s", err)
}

m, err := unix.Mmap(
    int(file.Fd()), 0, int(fi.Size()),
    unix.PROT_READ, unix.MAP_PRIVATE,
)
if err != nil {
    log.Fatalf("error: %s", err)
}
defer unix.Munmap(m) // free the mmap when done with it
```

Once you have a []byte, you can use bytes.Index to search for the loc: prefixes and parse the JSON found after them:

```
files/mmap/locs.go
pos := 0 // current position in data
locPrefix := []byte("loc:{")
var loc Location
for {
    i := bytes.Index(m[pos:], locPrefix) // find "loc:"
    if i == -1 {
        break
    }

    i += len(locPrefix) - 1 // move over "loc:"
    start := pos + i
    size := bytes.IndexByte(m[start:], '}') // find closing }
    if size == -1 {
        break
    }
    size++ // move over }

    if err := json.Unmarshal(m[start:start+size], &loc); err != nil {
        log.Fatalf("error: %s", err)
    }
    fmt.Printf("%+v\n", loc)
    pos = start + size + 1 // move after end of current JSON document
}
```

The following code will print:

```
{Lat:32.519585 Lng:35.015021}
{Lat:32.519606 Lng:35.014954}
{Lat:32.519612 Lng:35.014871}
{Lat:32.519654 Lng:35.014824}
...
```

The code works, and it works fast enough for the data pipeline to finish in time. You buy Joe a beer as a thank you and wonder if he ever buys his own beers.

Discussion

By using mmap and treating our data file as a []byte, we're able to write simpler code than we could have written by using an *os.File or io.Reader. This method will work, no matter the size of the file.

OS-Specific Solution

Using mmap is very specialized and operating-system specific. The preceding code will run only on Unix-like systems, such as Linux, OSX, and BSD. You'll need to write different code for Windows. Use build tags for OS-specific code. See *Using Build Tags for Conditional Builds* for more information.

Every time you need to work with data that's too big to fit in memory, think about mmap. If it's good enough for grep, it should be good enough for you.

Final Thoughts

This chapter covered how Go does a great job of abstracting I/O for us. Understanding how to use, and implement, these interfaces will help you easily deal with I/O.

You also saw how combining readers or writers on top of each other helps you write small pieces of code, each doing one simple thing.

Finally, we had a look at files, which are again part of the Unix way ("everything is a file").

Go tries to provide an operating-system-agnostic way of working with files. os.Open and friends should work regardless of the operating system, but in some edge cases, things will work differently.

Next, we're going to look at serialization, which is a way of passing data between programs.

## CHAPTER 2

Serializing Data

Serialization (or marshaling) is the act of taking a data structure in Go and converting it to a sequence of bytes. You'll use serialization at the "edges" of your program: when communicating with other programs over the network, when you store data to disk or database, and more.

Go has built-in support for several popular serializing formats, such as JSON, XML, and CSV. Go also has an internal gob serialization format, which is easier to work with but limited only to Go.

In this chapter, we'll cover several serialization formats but focus on one of the most popular serialization formats—JSON. The JSON serialization is textual without a schema, and it saves the type information in the serialized data so you can retrieve values with types without using an external schema.

JSON is a simple format, but it has some interesting edge cases—for example, handling timestamps. Due to the lack of schema, working with JSON in typed languages such as Go is challenging at times; JSON objects can be of any type, while the Go struct has a fixed set of fields with fixed types.

Recipe 8

Streaming Events with encoding/gob

Task

You're working with an online retailer, and they'd like to process events to understand customer behavior better.

You're tasked with writing both the client and handler code for events. And ... you're asked to deliver a prototype quickly.

Solution

You start by defining a generic Event interface which has a Kind:

serialize/events/events.go

```go
// Kind is event kind.
type Kind string

const (
    AddKind      Kind = "add"
    CheckoutKind Kind = "checkout"
)

type Event interface {
    Kind() Kind
}
```

Then you define two concrete events that implement the Event interface:

serialize/events/events.go

```go
// Add is an event of adding item to cart.
type Add struct {
    Time time.Time
    ID   string
    User string
    Item int // SKU
}

func (*Add) Kind() Kind {
    return AddKind
}

// Checkout is event for user checkout
type Checkout struct {
    Time time.Time
    Cart string
    User string
}

func (*Checkout) Kind() Kind {
    return CheckoutKind
}
```

And you register these types with encoding/gob so it'll know to encode/decode them as Event:

serialize/events/events.go
```go
func init() {
    gob.Register(&Add{})
    gob.Register(&Checkout{})
}
```

Now you write the encoder, which uses encoding/gob:

serialize/events/events.go
```go
Line 1  // Encoder is an event encoder.
   -    type Encoder struct {
   -        enc *gob.Encoder
   -    }
   5
   -    func NewEncoder(w io.Writer) *Encoder {
   -        return &Encoder{gob.NewEncoder(w)}
   -    }
   -
  10    func (e *Encoder) Encode(evt Event) error {
   -        return e.enc.Encode(&evt)
   -    }
```

And finally, the handler decodes an event and dispatches it to the right handler:

serialize/events/events.go
```go
func eventHandler(r io.Reader) error {
    dec := gob.NewDecoder(r)
    for {
        var e Event
        err := dec.Decode(&e)
        if err == io.EOF {
            break
        }
        if err != nil {
            return err
        }
        switch e.Kind() {
        case AddKind:
            handleAdd(e.(*Add))
        case CheckoutKind:
            handleCheckout(e.(*Checkout))
        default:
            return fmt.Errorf("unknown event kind: %s", e.Kind())
        }
    }
    return nil
}
```

Discussion

encoding/gob is a Go-specific format. It allows you to encode most of Go's types without adding special support for them in your types. But this works for Go only—applications written in other languages will have a very hard time communicating with your code.

When you serialize custom types using encoding/go, you need to use the same encoder to encode the whole stream. This limitation of using the same encoder is the reason you're using the Encoder types that have an enc field on line 3.

In line 11, you encode the *pointer* to the Event interface. If you encode the interface, and not the pointer to it, encoding/gob will encode the concrete type implementing the interface without the information about the interface.

Serializing is easy with encoding/gob, but you need to know how it works and be aware of some edge cases. Lucky for you, the documentation is excellent and contains several good examples. I highly encourage you to head over to https://golang.org/pkg/encoding/gob/. It's also got great examples of how to write Go documentation.

Recipe 9

Parsing Complex JSON Documents

Task

The online retailer you work for wants you to calculate the total number of purchases for a given time. Your company has a server for storing purchase information. This server has a REST API and will return a JSON document in the following format:

serialize/payments/reply.json
```json
{
  "payments": [
    {
      "id": 193,
      "date": "2020-03-17T13:03:02",
      "amount": 43.2
    },
    {
      "id": 197,
```

```
      "date": "2020-03-17T13:13:24",
      "amount": 59.6
    },
    {
      "id": 239,
      "date": "2020-03-17T16:42:17",
      "amount": 250.2
    }
  ]
}
```

In this recipe, we'll only cover parsing of the returned document. See Chapter 3, Utilizing HTTP, on page 37, for making HTTP calls.

Solution

You start by defining the parsing function signature:

```
serialize/payments/payments.go
func totalPayments(r io.Reader) (float64, error) {
```

Next, you define an anonymous struct with only the information you need:

```
serialize/payments/payments.go
var reply struct {
    Payments []struct {
        Amount float64
    }
}
```

Then you use encoding/json to decode the data into the reply struct:

```
serialize/payments/payments.go
if err := json.NewDecoder(r).Decode(&reply); err != nil {
    return 0, err
}
```

Finally, when the data is in reply, you can calculate the total amount:

```
serialize/payments/payments.go
total := 0.0
for _, p := range reply.Payments {
    total += p.Amount
}
return total, nil
```

Discussion

When unmarshaling, encoding/json will populate struct fields and ignore all other fields in the incoming JSON document.

Since encoding/json ignores unknown fields, it means you don't need to model the *whole* structure of the returned document but only the fields you need.

Since reply is specific to the totalPayments function, there's no need to define a named type for it (meaning type Reply struct { ...}—you use an anonymous struct and avoid namespace pollution.

reply is an anonymous struct, but you still need to export (start with an uppercase letter) the fields you'd like encoding/json to populate.

Usually, field names in the JSON document are all lowercase. encoding/json has some heuristics on how to map from JSON names to struct field names (Amount ↔ amount). If you'll encode struct to JSON, the field names will start with an uppercase. You can use field tags to let the JSON encoder/decoder know the right mapping from Go to JSON names.

Here's an example:

```
serialize/user.go
// User is a user message.
type User struct {
    Name string `json:"login"`
    ID   int    `json:"uid"`
}
```

Recipe 10

Streaming JSON

Task

Your company has a centralized logging server. To ingest logs, you need to connect to a socket, and then it'll stream the log message, one per line, in JSON format.

A log line looks like this:

```
{"Time":"2020-10-28T15:42:39.164085279+02:00","Level":20,"Message":"DB is up"}
```

You need to write a function that will listen on the socket, parse the JSON messages, and pass them to a handler function.

Solution

You start by writing the function signature:

serialize/stream/stream.go
```
func ingestLogs(r io.Reader, handler func(Log)) error {
```

Then you create an encoding/json.Decoder:

serialize/stream/stream.go
```
dec := json.NewDecoder(r)
```

Now you can run a for loop, consuming one JSON object at a time and passing it to the handler function in line 12:

serialize/stream/stream.go
```
Line 1  for {
            var l Log
            err := dec.Decode(&l)
            if err == io.EOF {
     5          break
            }

            if err != nil {
                return err
    10      }

            handler(l)
        }
```

And finally, once you encounter an io.EOF error, you return nil:

serialize/stream/stream.go
```
return nil
```

Discussion

The JSON protocol does not support streaming of objects. You can decode or encode only one object at a time.

Inside the for loop, you create a new Log struct on every iteration (line 2). You might consider reusing an existing struct to save some memory, but you need to be careful and zero out all the fields in the struct before you reuse it. I find it easier and less error prone to use the current approach of creating a new Log struct every time. Services that want to stream JSON usually do it by sending one JSON object per line. The encoding/json decoder is aware of this practice and will consume one object at a time from an io.Reader.

The pattern of having an ingestion function that handles incoming messages and passes to a handler function is very common. You can find this pattern in net/http web servers, gRPC, and other frameworks.

In his book *The Art of Unix Programming*, Eric S. Raymond calls this pattern the Rule of Separation: separate policy from mechanism; separate interfaces from engines.

Recipe 11

Handling Missing Values in JSON

Task

The company you work for has a centralized logging system. On every server is an agent that tails the log file and sends new logs over HTTP to the central logging system. A log struct looks like this:

serialize/missing/missing.go
```go
// Log is a log event.
type Log struct {
    Time    time.Time
    Level   int
    Message string
}
```

When you come back from lunch one day, you see the following issue assigned to you:

```
In some cases we see that the log level is 0, which is an invalid level.
In other cases, we see the time as January 1, 1.
```

You love a good mystery, so you dig in.

Solution

You start by looking at some raw log data (which you saved just for a case like this) and find out that in some logs, fields are missing or misspelled. This information gives you a lead to the problem.

Go initializes every struct field to its zero value, so suppose you create an empty log:

```go
var l Log
```

The value of the Level field will be the zero value for int, which is 0, and the zero value for Time will be January 1, 1.

You come with this finding to your team leader, and he says you need to reject invalid input, such as missing fields.

You create a parseLog function. It uses an internal anonymous structure with pointer fields and then checks if these fields are nil:

serialize/missing/missing.go
```go
func parseLog(data []byte) (*Log, error) {
    var l struct {
        Time    *time.Time
        Level   *int
        Message string
    }
    if err := json.Unmarshal(data, &l); err != nil {
        return nil, err
    }

    if l.Time == nil {
        return nil, fmt.Errorf("missing `time` field")
    }

    if l.Level == nil {
        return nil, fmt.Errorf("missing `level` field")
    }

    if l.Message == "" {
        return nil, fmt.Errorf("missing `message` field")
    }

    return &Log{*l.Time, *l.Level, l.Message}, nil
}
```

Discussion

It's for good reason that Go is initializing variables and fields to their zero values—it creates predictable code that is less error prone. But it creates a problem when you need to know if a zero value comes from user input or from missing input.

In the current solution, you turn the Time and Level fields to pointers, and when you get a nil value, you *know* it's missing user input.

The downside of this method is that you now copy the data twice in the parsing code, once into l and then into the returned Log. In speed- or memory-intensive applications, this approach might be a problem.

The upside is that the user-facing Log doesn't use pointers, which makes it easier to work with—no need to dereference pointers or check for nil values.

Recipe 12

Serializing Custom Types

Task

You're working on a collaborative online code editor. The editor uses a stack to keep track of open/close parentheses so it'll be able to highlight matching ones.

Your code has a Stack data type that's defined as follows:

serialize/stack/stack.go
```
// Stack is a LIFO data structure.
type Stack struct {
    Value string
    Next  *Stack
}
```

To collaborate with other editors, you need to send a stack to another service using JSON and also receive stacks from other services.

Solution

To support JSON marshaling, you implement the encoding/json.Marshaler interface:

serialize/stack/stack.go
```
Line 1  // MarshalJSON implements json.Marshaler.
     2  func (s *Stack) MarshalJSON() ([]byte, error) {
     3      var values []string
     4      for s != nil {
     5          values = append(values, s.Value)
     6          s = s.Next
     7      }
     8
     9      return json.Marshal(values)
    10  }
```

And to support unmarshaling, you implement the encoding/json.Unmarshaler interface:

serialize/stack/stack.go

```
Line 1   // UnmarshalJSON implements json.Unmarshaler.
     -   func (s *Stack) UnmarshalJSON(data []byte) error {
     -       var values []string
     -       if err := json.Unmarshal(data, &values); err != nil {
     5           return err
     -       }
     -
     -       var node *Stack
     -       for i := len(values) - 1; i >= 0; i-- {
    10           node = &Stack{values[i], node}
     -       }
     -
     -       *s = *node
     -       return nil
    15   }
```

Discussion

The JSON format supports a very limited set of types. These are mapped to the following Go types:

JSON Type	Go Type
Array	[]any
Boolean	bool
null	nil
Number	float64
Object	map[string]any
String	string

When serializing a custom type, consider which JSON type is the closest.

In our case, you chose Array as the type you'd like to use in JSON.

Once you convert the custom type to a type JSON can process, use the built-in encoding/json.Marshal to convert it to JSON.

In our code, once the stack is converted to a slice, you use encoding/json.Marshal to finish the conversion in line 9.

When unmarshaling, you need to implement UnmarshalJSON on a pointer receiver. Make sure to update the pointer value and not the pointer itself, like you do in line 13.

Several other serialization packages take the same approach. The secret is to find which interface to implement; for example, in the external YAML package you need to implement MarshalYAML and UnmarshalYAML. I think you get the idea of which interfaces and methods to look for.

Unmarshaling Dynamic Types

Task

You are in charge of a web server that gets notification events over HTTP. The events are encoded in JSON format but have various types.

Your team lead, Alice, asks you to start by supporting a Login and a Message type, defined as follows:

serialize/dynamic/dynamic.go
```
// Login is a login event.
type Login struct {
    User    int // user ID
    Success bool
}

// Message is a message event.
type Message struct {
    From int // user ID
    To   int // user ID
    Text string
}
```

In each JSON object is a type field that tells you the type of the object.

Solution

You decode to write a specific handler per message type, and then you write a generic handler function that will dispatch messages:

serialize/dynamic/dynamic.go
```
func handler(data []byte) error {
```

First you unmarshal the data into a map[string]any:

serialize/dynamic/dynamic.go
```
var obj map[string]any
if err := json.Unmarshal(data, &obj); err != nil {
    return err
}
```

Then you grab the type field from the message:

```
serialize/dynamic/dynamic.go
val, ok := obj["type"]
if !ok {
    return fmt.Errorf("missing `type` in %+v", obj)
}

typ, ok := val.(string)
if !ok {
    return fmt.Errorf("`type` is not a string - %v of %T", val, val)
}
```

Once you have the type as a string, you can dispatch it:

```
serialize/dynamic/dynamic.go
switch typ {
case "login":
    var l Login
    if err := mapstructure.Decode(obj, &l); err != nil {
        return err
    }
    return handleLogin(l)
case "message":
    var m Message
    if err := mapstructure.Decode(obj, &m); err != nil {
        return err
    }
    return handleMessage(m)
default:
    return fmt.Errorf("unknown message type: %q", typ)
}
```

Discussion

You can use map[string]any to decode any arbitrary JSON object. However, working directly with this type requires a lot of type assertions—the code very quickly becomes ugly. Just see how much work you do just to extract the type field as a string.

Once you unmarshal JSON to map[string]any, you can use github.com/mitchellh/mapstructure to unmarshal this map to a concrete structure.

This approach requires two serializations instead of one, but there's not much else you can do when working with dynamic messages. JSON is great for dynamically typed languages such as JavaScript or Python, but in typed languages such as Go, you'll need to work harder to handle this lack of structure.

Recipe 14

Parsing Struct Tags

Task

You're building an ORM (object-relational mapper) for your company's proprietary database. An ORM simplifies working with the database—you store and retrieve Go structs directly instead of using []any.

Your first task is to parse a user struct and return the mapping between the field names and the database columns. Take the following struct, for example:

serialize/orm/orm.go
```
// Log is a log structure.
type Log struct {
    Time  time.Time `db:"ts"`
    Level int       `db:"level"`
    Text  string    `db:"message"`
}
```

You should return the mapping of the following:

- Time → ts
- Level → level
- Text → message

Solution

You start by defining the parsing function signature:

serialize/orm/orm.go
```
func parseStructTags(s any) (map[string]string, error) {
```

First, you use the reflect package to get the type of the parameter:

serialize/orm/orm.go
```
typ := reflect.TypeOf(s)
if typ.Kind() != reflect.Struct {
    return nil, fmt.Errorf("%s is not a struct", typ)
}
```

Then you iterate over the struct fields and extract the db key from the field tag:

serialize/orm/orm.go

```
m := make(map[string]string)
for i := 0; i < typ.NumField(); i++ {
    fld := typ.Field(i)
    if dbName := fld.Tag.Get("db"); dbName != "" {
        m[fld.Name] = dbName
    }
}
return m, nil
```

Discussion

Since parseStructTags should accept any value, the type of its parameter is any. Most of the time, using any is a "code smell" and you should use concrete types or an interface.

However, in this case, you can't use a concrete type or an interface, so you're left with using any.

(Note: the term *code smell* was coined by Kent Beck and means a surface indication that usually corresponds to a deeper problem in the system.)

Struct tags are used by many serialization packages; the built-in encoding/json, encoding/xml, and many other external packages, such as yaml, use them.

Struct tags allow you to add extra information about a field. They have a known format: key:"value" key:"value" .... The Field type in the reflect package has methods to extract a specific key.

In some cases, the value can be more than just a name. Commonly, it's either a list of values separated by a , or a name=value. Here's an example from a struct generated by Google's protoc tool:

```
Value float64 `protobuf:"fixed64,1,opt,name=value,proto3" \
    json:"value,omitempty"`
```

The struct tag has two keys: protobuf and json, and both have complex values.

If you decide you need complex values (like protobuf in our example), you need to design the format used in these tags since you're basically implementing your own serialization format.

It's best to copy what encoding/json or protobuf are doing instead of inventing your own.

Final Thoughts

Serialization seems like a simple concept: take a value in Go and convert it to a sequence of bytes. But there are a lot of edge cases.

And since serialization formats support multiple languages, there are translation problems.

We looked mainly at JSON since it's the most popular serialization format; however, many other serialization formats are available (for example, Protocol Buffers). If you can, run a proof of concept on several formats before you commit to one. The criteria for picking a format vary from team to team, but some factors include:

- Performance (both speed and number of bytes)
- Supported types (for example, JSON is missing a timestamp type)
- Language support
- Schema support

You'll find a lot of what we covered here—streaming, missing values, unsupported types, and more—in other serialization formats. Whatever format you use, make sure to learn it thoroughly so you can work with it efficiently. (Just don't pick CSV—it's a horrible format.)

Next, we'll look at the HTTP protocol and how you can write clients and servers.

## CHAPTER 3

Utilizing HTTP

HTTP is *the* protocol people use for passing data around. It's a simple, text-oriented protocol, but you need to consider many fine points when working with it—for example, chunked encoding.

Lucky for you, the built-in net/http package is production ready and packed with features.

In this chapter, we'll look at ways to perform common, and maybe not-so-common, tasks using the HTTP protocol. We'll look at streaming (chunked-encoding) requests, using middleware, setting timeouts, and more.

Recipe 15

Making GET Requests

Task

Your team is using GitHub for hosting your code. As part of an effort to improve the development process, you are asked to provide some metrics on the project. Your first task is to list the currently open pull requests (PRs).

After spending some time reading the GitHub API with documentation, you find out that you need to:

- Construct a URL in the format /repos/{owner}/{repo}/pulls
- Set the Content-Type header to application/vnd.github.v3+json
- Pass state=open as an HTTP query parameter

The response is a JSON document in the following format:

http/pulls/reply_example.json
```json
[
  {
    "number": 138,
    "state": "open",
    "title": "Add option to filter by date",
    ...
  },
  {
    "number": 297,
    "state": "open",
    "title": "Moving average calculation fails with missing data (nan)",
    ...
  },
  ...
]
```

The API is paginated, meaning it won't return all the results at once. You need to pass a page HTTP query parameter, starting from 1 and going on until you don't get any more results.

Solution

You start by writing code to build a URL from owner, repo, and the requested page.

http/pulls/pulls.go
```go
func buildURL(owner, repo string, page int) string {
    // We want only open PRs to master
    query := url.Values{}
    query.Set("state", "open")
    query.Set("base", "master")
    query.Set("per_page", "100")
    query.Set("page", fmt.Sprintf("%d", page))

    owner, repo = url.PathEscape(owner), url.PathEscape(repo)
    const format = "https://api.github.com/repos/%s/%s/pulls?%s"
    return fmt.Sprintf(format, owner, repo, query.Encode())
}
```

You also need code to parse a response:

http/pulls/pulls.go
```go
// PR is pull request info.
type PR struct {
    Number int
    Title  string
}

func parseResponse(r io.Reader) ([]PR, error) {
    var prs []PR
    if err := json.NewDecoder(r).Decode(&prs); err != nil {
```

```
        return nil, err
    }

    return prs, nil
}
```

Now you can write the code to fetch one page of results:

http/pulls/pulls.go

```
func pageOpenPRs(owner, repo string, page int) ([]PR, error) {
    url := buildURL(owner, repo, page)

    ctx, cancel := context.WithTimeout(context.Background(), 10*time.Second)
    defer cancel()
    req, err := http.NewRequestWithContext(ctx, "GET", url, nil)
    if err != nil {
        return nil, err
    }
    req.Header.Set("Accept", "application/vnd.github.v3+json")

    resp, err := http.DefaultClient.Do(req)
    if err != nil {
        return nil, err
    } else if resp.StatusCode != http.StatusOK {
        const format = "bad status: %d - %s"
        return nil, fmt.Errorf(format, resp.StatusCode, resp.Status)
    }
    log.Printf("URL: %s", url)

    defer resp.Body.Close()
    r := io.LimitReader(resp.Body, 10*(1<<20)) // Don't read more than 10MB
    return parseResponse(r)
}
```

And finally, you can get all of the open pull requests:

http/pulls/pulls.go

```
func openPRs(owner, repo string) ([]PR, error) {
    var prs []PR
    for page := 1; true; page++ {
        pagePRs, err := pageOpenPRs(owner, repo, page)
        if err != nil {
            return nil, err
        }

        if len(pagePRs) == 0 {
            break
        }
        prs = append(prs, pagePRs...)
    }

    return prs, nil
}
```

Discussion

You can pass arguments to HTTP requests in three places:

- HTTP parameter in the request URL
- HTTP header in the request headers
- The request body

In the buildURL function, you handle the parameters passed in the URL. You should never "handcraft" the URL by using the functions in the fmt package. When building URLs, special characters need to be escaped, and there are other considerations as well.

Most HTTP GET requests don't contain a body. When there's no body, you pass nil as the last parameter to NewRequestWithContext.

The network isn't reliable, so you need to protect yourself as much as you can. In this code, you use a context.Context to limit the amount of time the HTTP request takes. This will help with network glitches.

Retry Logic

You might consider adding a *retry logic* to your requests. Retry is trickier than it seems; you need to think about the number of times you retry until you give up. You also need to think about the pauses between retries.

Take a look at https://github.com/hashicorp/go-retryablehttp for an example implementation.

The network is also not secure, so you should protect yourself as much as you can. You're using io.LimitReader to limit the amount of data you read into memory, which is one way to protect yourself against malicious agents (say, someone sending back 100 GB).

Recipe 16

Streaming POST Requests

Task

You work with the devops team to help with server visibility. Jenny, the team lead, asks you to create a client that will send metrics, such as CPU load, to a central HTTP server that will collect the results.

A metric is defined as follows:

```
http/stream/metrics.go
// Metric is a metric in the system.
type Metric struct {
    Name   string    `json:"name"`
    Host   string    `json:"host"`
    Time   time.Time `json:"time"`
    Value  float64   `json:"value"`
}
```

Another team member already wrote the function that collects the metrics:

```
http/stream/metrics.go
func collectMetrics() <-chan Metric {
```

Solution

You start by writing a producer function that will encode the metrics from collectMetrics as JSON into an io.WriteCloser:

```
http/stream/metrics.go
func producer(w io.WriteCloser) {
    defer w.Close()

    enc := json.NewEncoder(w)
    for m := range collectMetrics() {
        if err := enc.Encode(m); err != nil {
            log.Printf("error: can't encode %#v - %s", m, err)
            return
        }
    }
}
```

And then you write updateMetrics:

http/stream/metrics.go
```
func updateMetrics() error {
    r, w, err := os.Pipe()
    if err != nil {
        return err
    }

    go producer(w)

    req, err := http.NewRequest("POST", serverURL, r)
    if err != nil {
        return err
    }

    resp, err := http.DefaultClient.Do(req)
    if err != nil {
        return err
    }
    if resp.StatusCode != http.StatusOK {
        const format = "bad reply status: %d %s"
        return fmt.Errorf(format, resp.StatusCode, resp.Status)
    }

    return nil
}
```

Discussion

You use os.Pipe to create a read and a write side. The write side is sent to producer, which encodes the metrics, and the read side is sent at the request body to http.NewRequest. The producer *must* close the write side to signal there's no more data available.

Go will use HTTP chunked transfer encoding to send the data.

Chunked Transfer Encoding

 Chunked transfer encoding was added in HTTP version 1.1. When using this method, the body is sent in chunks: the client first sends the size of the chunk and then the chunk data itself. Unlike "regular" HTTP requests, you don't specify the size of the data in advance.

See more at https://developer.mozilla.org/en-US/docs/Web/HTTP/Headers/Transfer-Encoding.

Streaming data using HTTP chunked encoding is a good option when you don't know the size of generated data in advance or when the data is very big and you don't want to hold it in memory.

Recipe 17

Writing Middleware to Monitor Performance

Task

Some users are complaining that your company's website feels sluggish. The operations team wants to find out if there's a performance problem and uncover its origin. They ask you to add log entries for several handlers that will record the time it took each handler to run.

Solution

You start by writing a middleware to add logging:

```
http/log_middleware/httpd.go
// addLogging is a middleware that adds logging to a handler.
func addLogging(name string, handler http.Handler) http.Handler {
    wrapper := func(w http.ResponseWriter, r *http.Request) {
        start := time.Now()

        handler.ServeHTTP(w, r)

        duration := time.Since(start)
        log.Printf("%s took %s", name, duration)
    }

    return http.HandlerFunc(wrapper)
}
```

And then you use it to wrap a handler:

```
http/log_middleware/httpd.go
hdlr := addLogging("query", http.HandlerFunc(queryHandler))
http.Handle("/query", hdlr)
```

Discussion

A middleware is a function that gets an http.Handler, and possibly some more parameters, and returns an http.Handler. The middleware "wraps" the original http.Handler passed to it and adds some functionality. This functionality can be before the original handler is called, say, to validate authentication, or after the handler is called, like you do in addLogging.

The net/http package enables writing middleware by using the http.Handler interface in most functions.

Using addLogging middleware instead of writing the timing and logging code directly in the handler function keeps the handler simple and focused on what it does.

Several external HTTP frameworks, such as chi and others, provide middleware function for common tasks like logging, recovery, and more.

Recipe 18

Setting Server Timeouts

Task

The operations team is facing some erratic network behavior. They're working to fix it. But in the meantime, they ask you to add timeouts to your HTTP server. These timeouts will make sure that the server doesn't get "stuck" on network reading or writing.

Solution

You start by defining an http.Server and setting ReadTimeout and WriteTimeout:

```
http/timeouts/httpd.go
srv := http.Server{
    Addr:        ":8080",
    Handler:     http.DefaultServeMux,
    ReadTimeout:  3 * time.Second,
    WriteTimeout: 2 * time.Second,
}
```

Then, instead of running http.ListenAndServe, you call the srv.ListenAndServe method:

```
http/timeouts/httpd.go
if err := srv.ListenAndServe(); err != nil {
    log.Fatalf("error: %s", err)
}
```

Discussion

I'll probably repeat myself, but it's an important point: the network is *not* reliable. You should set timeouts on every network call you make. Setting timeouts will prevent network operations from getting stuck and will also guard you against malicious uses.

You'll find several timeouts you can define on the built-in http.Server. The two most used are ReadTimeout and WriteTimeout. The following image shows what each of them covers:

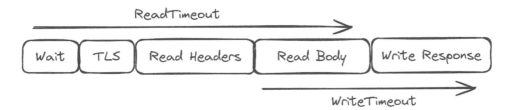

When you define your own http.Server, you also need to give it the address to listen on and the main http.Handler to pass requests to. In our case, we use the http.DefaultServeMux as the handler, allowing us to use the usual http.HandleFunc and friends.

Don't forget to test your server against timeouts. It might be tricky, but it's worth the effort—you'll sleep sounder at night knowing a flaky network won't trigger your beeper at 2 a.m. See *Testing Your Code* to get some testing ideas.

Recipe 19

Supporting Several API Versions in the Same HTTP Server

Task

Your dog-walking service is a huge success—many customers are using it to schedule walks for their dogs.

You start to realize that to support growth, you must change the server REST API to reduce the number of calls clients make to your side.

You decide to write a version 2 of the server REST API, but to enable smooth migration, you want to serve both version 1 and version 2 for a migration period.

Solution

You decide that clients who want version 2 of the API must specify X-API-ver HTTP header with the value of 2.

You start by separating the handlers and routers for version 1 and version 2.

Here's the code for the old version 1 API:

http/apiver/httpd.go
```
func v1HealthHandler(w http.ResponseWriter, r *http.Request) {
    w.Write([]byte("OK (v1)\n"))
}

func v1Mux() *http.ServeMux {
    mux := http.NewServeMux()
    mux.HandleFunc("/health", v1HealthHandler)
    return mux
}
```

And here's the code for the shiny new version 2 of the API:

http/apiver/httpd.go
```
func v2HealthHandler(w http.ResponseWriter, r *http.Request) {
    w.Write([]byte("OK (v2)\n"))
}

func v2Mux() *http.ServeMux {
    mux := http.NewServeMux()
    mux.HandleFunc("/_/health", v2HealthHandler)
    return mux
}
```

Now you can write main, which will dispatch requests depending on the X-API-ver header:

http/apiver/httpd.go
```
func main() {
    v1 := v1Mux()
    v2 := v2Mux()

    versionRouter := func(w http.ResponseWriter, r *http.Request) {
        if r.Header.Get("X-API-ver") == "2" {
            v2.ServeHTTP(w, r)
        } else {
            v1.ServeHTTP(w, r)
        }
    }
    http.HandleFunc("/", versionRouter)

    addr := ":8080"
    log.Printf("info: server ready on %s", addr)
    if err := http.ListenAndServe(addr, nil); err != nil {
        log.Fatalf("error: %s", err)
    }
}
```

Next you run some tests, and you first see the default API is still version 1:

```
$ curl http://localhost:8080/health
OK (v1)
$ curl http://localhost:8080/_/health
404 page not found
```

And then you can check that version 2 is served when you set the X-API-ver HTTP header:

```
$ curl -H 'X-API-ver: 2' http://localhost:8080/_/health
OK (v2)
$ curl -H 'X-API-ver: 2' http://localhost:8080/health
404 page not found
```

You're ready to roll out version 2 of your API.

Discussion

Changing an API is a serious decision. Once your API is published, customers will start using it and depending on it. You need to be very conservative when changing APIs and give your users a very long time to migrate. One of the reasons Go is successful is due to its compatibility promise.[1] I had the pleasure of going through the Python 2 to Python 3 migration, and even though the changes weren't that big, it took about eight years for most companies and projects to migrate.

Some developers prefer to use a /v1 prefix from the first API release, paving the path to version 2, which might never come.

Final Thoughts

In this chapter, we covered some practical points of using the HTTP protocol.

If you're developing servers, mostly with REST APIs, you should invest time and learn about the HTTP protocol. The net/http package should have your back on most of the tasks you'll need to perform.

But in some cases, external libraries such as chi and friends can make your life easier, especially when you need fancier routing by HTTP methods and some path variables. Adding external packages is always a risk—make sure the value you get from these packages is worth the risk.

Next on the list is the surprisingly tricky topic of working with text.

---

1. https://golang.org/doc/go1compat

## CHAPTER 4

Working with Text

To rephrase Doug McIlroy, "Text is the universal interface." Text looks like a simple topic ... until you get to Unicode.

Unicode gives you the ability to handle many human languages in your code. Unicode can be confusing though, and developers love to hate it.

Go supports Unicode from the ground up. The following recipes will show you a pragmatic approach for, as much as possible, painless development with Unicode.

Apart from processing text, we'll also discuss how to present text in a way that helps us humans understand what's going on.

Recipe 20

Using Formatting Verbs for Better Output

Task

You've decided to enter the hot ride-hailing market. To find the car nearest a customer, you need to keep track of where your cars are located. Every minute, your cars are sending a LocationEvent. You'd like to log these events so you can come up with better algorithms to find rides closer to your customers.

Solution

You start by defining a LocationEvent struct:

```
text/fmt/log/log.go
// LocationEvent is a location event.
type LocationEvent struct {
    ID        string
    Latitude  float64
    Longitude float64
}
```

Then you create an Event:

```
text/fmt/log/log.go
evt := &LocationEvent{
    ID:        "McQueen95",
    Latitude:  40.7060361,
    Longitude: -74.0110143,
}
```

You're using the built-in log package to log the event:

```
text/fmt/log/log.go
log.Printf("info: loc: %#v", evt)
```

It prints the following:

```
$ go run log.go
2023/07/05 17:19:48 info: loc: &main.LocationEvent{\
    ID:"McQueen95", Latitude:40.7060361, Longitude:-74.0110143}
```

Discussion

The log package uses the same formatting verbs as the fmt package. This means the formatting strings are the same in both packages.

In the following examples, I'll use the fmt package since it produces simpler output than the log package, which will make the examples clearer and easier to follow.

In your applications, you should use the log package; it allows the user of your code to decide where to send the logs, in contrast to the fmt package, which prints to standard output (or an io.Writer).

Logging Format

 You can control the format of the log package output (for example, the timestamp prefix) using the log.SetFlags() function.[1]

---

1. https://golang.org/pkg/log/#SetFlags

The %v verb is *the value in a default format.* You can use it to print any type, which is handy when debugging and logging. It has two optional flags: + (which we use) and #.

Let's see the differences between + and #:

```
text/fmt/v/v.go
fmt.Printf("%v\n", evt)
// &{McQueen95 40.7060361 -74.0110143}
fmt.Printf("%+v\n", evt)
// &{ID:McQueen95 Latitude:40.7060361 Longitude:-74.0110143}
fmt.Printf("%#v\n", evt)
// &main.LocationEvent{ID:"McQueen95", Latitude:40.7060361, \
//     Longitude:-74.0110143}
```

The + flag adds the field names next to their values, and the # flag adds the type information as well. It's great for developers, but probably not that great for end users.

When logging (or debugging), I use the # flag and encourage you to do the same.

The #v formatting verb is handy not only in structs but also with other types:

```
text/fmt/v/v.go
id1, id2 := 1, "1"
fmt.Printf("id1=%v id2=%v\n", id1, id2)   // id1=1 id2=1
fmt.Printf("id1=%#v id2=%#v\n", id1, id2) // id1=1 id2="1"
```

In the preceding example, a is an int, while b is a string. When you use the %v verb, the values of a and b look the same, which makes debugging hard. With the %#v you can see the difference in the type.

The fmt (and log) package has several verbs, each with its options flags and directives.

I encourage you to learn their capabilities—verbs are well documented in the fmt package documentation. When printing, think about which verb will make your output clearer.

Recipe 21

Adding String Representation to Your Types

Task

You're working on a bug-tracking system that everybody will finally love. You start simple, and start with bugs that have only a title and a priority. To save space, you decide to make the priority a uint8. You'd like to have the priority name, not the numeric value, printed out when printing a bug.

Solution

You start by defining a Priority type and define some concrete values:

text/fmt/level/level.go
```
// Priority is bug priority.
type Priority uint8

const (
    Low     Priority = 10
    Medium Priority = 20
    High    Priority = 30
)
```

To add custom string formatting, you implement the fmt.Stringer[2] interface:

text/fmt/level/level.go
```
// String implements the fmt.Stringer interface.
func (p Priority) String() string {
    switch p {
    case Low:
        return "low"
    case Medium:
        return "medium"
    case High:
        return "high"
    }
    return fmt.Sprintf("<%d>", p)
}
```

Now you can use Priority in our Bug struct:

---

2.   https://golang.org/pkg/fmt/#Stringer

```
text/fmt/level/level.go
// Bug is a bug in the system.
type Bug struct {
    Title    string
    Priority Priority
}
```

And finally, you test out your code:

```
text/fmt/level/level.go
func main() {
    bug := Bug{"Bug level is printed as number", Medium}
    fmt.Printf("%+v\n", bug)
    // {Title:Bug level is printed as number Priority:medium}
}
```

Discussion

When the fmt gets a value to print, it'll use reflection to see if the value's type implements the fmt.Stringer interface.

If this type does implement the interface, fmt will use the type String method instead of the default formatting for this value.

Here's how you might code this logic:

```
text/fmt/stringer/stringer.go
func formatValue(val any) string {
    if s, ok := val.(fmt.Stringer); ok { // val implements fmt.Stringer
        return s.String()
    }

    // Return default formatting ...
    switch val.(type) {
    // TODO ...
    }
```

Try commenting out the String method and rerunning the code. Now you'll see the output:

```
{Title:Bug level is printed as number Priority:20}
```

The Priority field is printed with the default format for uint8.

In the String method, we use a switch statement to check for the predefined priorities. If we reach the highlighted line, it means we have an unknown priority, and we return a generic number value.

Be careful not to use the %s or %v since in this case it'll cause an infinite recursion (I encourage you to figure out why).

You can see this behavior by changing the Priority in the highlighted line in main function at fmt/level.go from Medium to Priority(7).

Note that if you use the %#v format, you'll see a different output:

```
main.Bug{Title:"Bug level is printed as number", Priority:0x14}
```

To control how %#v is printed, either implement the fmt.GoStringer interface or the fmt.Formatter interface.

By implementing fmt.Stringer in your types, you can make sure they are printed nicely with the fmt or log packages.

Recipe 22

Detecting Encoding

Task: Detecting Encoding

You're working in a cyber security company. One of the products you provide is scanning the client site and checking to see if any sensitive information is out in the open. Jessie, your team member, wrote the crawler that travels the client website. For each web page, the crawler returns its content in a []byte format. Your team lead asks you to convert the []byte to string so you'll be able to search the data.

Screen Scraping

 Crawling over a site's web pages is called "screen scraping." It should be the last resort, and you should look for a programmable API first. I've written several such systems, and they are very brittle. It's enough that the website changes a template and everything breaks.

These days, a lot of sites load page elements using JavaScript, and you'll need to use tools such as Selenium or Playwright. These tools come with a big operational overhead.

Solution

The easy path is when the server returns a Content-Type HTTP header with the encoding:

```
text/detect/detect.go
// ctypeEncoding gets encoding from HTTP Content-Type header
func ctypeEncoding(ctype string) string {
    _, params, err := mime.ParseMediaType(ctype)
    if err != nil {
        return ""
    }
    return params["charset"]
}
```

Then, if there's no header, you use the golang.org/x/net/html/charset package to detect the encoding:

```
text/detect/detect.go
func dataEncoding(data []byte) string {
    _, name, certain := charset.DetermineEncoding(data, "text/plain")
    if certain {
        return name
    }
    return ""
}
```

Finally, you quickly test the code with a main that first tries the easy path of Content-Type and then reads the data and finds the encoding:

```
text/detect/detect.go
resp, err := http.Get(url)
if err != nil {
    log.Fatalf("error: %s", err)
}
defer resp.Body.Close()

enc := ctypeEncoding(resp.Header.Get("Content-Type"))
if enc != "" {
    fmt.Printf("Content-Type encoding is %s\n", enc)
    os.Exit(0)
}

data, err := io.ReadAll(resp.Body)
if err != nil {
    log.Fatalf("error: %s", err)
}

enc = dataEncoding(data)
if enc != "" {
    fmt.Printf("detected encoding is %s\n", enc)
    os.Exit(0)
}

fmt.Println("can't detect encoding")
os.Exit(1)
```

You try it out:

```
$ go run detect.go https://www.gutenberg.org/files/76/76-0.txt
2020/05/24 19:03:22 getting https://www.gutenberg.org/files/76/76-0.txt
detected encoding is utf-8
```

Discussion

At the program edges, you'll get a chunk of bytes, or a []byte. When you want to convert them to a string, you'll need to know the encoding.

When working with HTTP, you can use the Content-Type header:

```
$ curl -si https://github.com | head -4
HTTP/2 200
server: GitHub.com
date: Tue, 26 Apr 2022 09:51:07 GMT
content-type: text/html; charset=utf-8
```

GitHub returned Content-Type header of text/html; charset=utf-8, which means you are getting HTML encoded in UTF-8.

In other cases, you'll need to guess the encoding. golang.org/x/net/html/charset is a package that provides a way to guess the encoding of a []byte. It'll return an encoding and a flag saying if it's certain or not.

To put what you've learned here to use, I encourage you to go over your existing code and try to find places where you mistreat Unicode or have Unicode-related potential bugs—and fix them.

Recipe 23

Using Regular Expressions to Convert camelCase to lower_with_underscore

Task

Your company collects a lot of data for its data science team. The data engineering team needs help, and you volunteer since you want to gain some experience in this area. You get an email from the data engineering lead:

> Hi and welcome to the team. Your first task is to help us normalize fields in our data pipeline. We'd like you to write a code that converts fields from camelCase

to lower_with_underscore. Feel free to approach me if you have any questions. Good luck!

You start by reading the data engineering documentation and then set to work.

Solution

You start by defining a regular expression that captures a lowercase letter followed by an uppercase letter:

text/camel/etl.go
```
var (
    // Example: match "rN" in "userName"
    camelRe = regexp.MustCompile(`[a-z][A-Z]`)
)
```

Then you write a function that gives a two-letter string, returns the first letter, then an _, and then the second letter in lowercase:

text/camel/etl.go
```
// fixCase gets a string in the format "aB" and return "a_b"
func fixCase(s string) string {
    return fmt.Sprintf("%c_%c", s[0], unicode.ToLower(rune(s[1])))
}
```

Finally, you can use fixCase with the camelRe regular expressions ReplaceAllStringFunc method.

text/camel/etl.go
```
// camelToLower turns "camelCase" to "camel_case"
func camelToLower(s string) string {
    return camelRe.ReplaceAllStringFunc(s, fixCase)
}
```

Discussion

You start by constructing camelRe once in a var expression. Since you can't check for errors inside the var expression, you use the MustCompile function, which will panic on an invalid regular expression. This might seem unsafe, since the error will happen at runtime, but since you *do* have tests—they will fail before your code goes to production.

Regular Expressions

 Adding some input examples next to a regular expression makes it much easier to understand. You can use sites such as https://regex101.com/ to test your regular expressions.

The regexp.Regexp struct implements many methods. You chose to use the ReplaceAllStringFunc, which calls a function on every match and returns a new string where all matches are replaced with the function return value.

Regular expressions are a powerful tool, but they have many edge cases, so you need to know how to work with them. In this example, using a function for substitution made the code simpler and easier to maintain.

Recipe 24

Folding Strings for Case-Insensitive Comparison

Task

You just got funded to create a company that offers culinary tours in cities. You sit down and start coding.

The first task is to search for a city in a database of tours, each with time, city, and name. Initially, you'd like to have the ability to search for tours at a certain city.

When people use search engines, they usually don't care about the case of words. They'll search for Gdańsk or gdańsk and expect the same results. We'd like to have the same functionality in our system and write code that searches for a city regardless of the case of the query string.

Solution

You start by defining a Tour struct:

text/tours/fold/tours.go
```go
// Tour is a tour in a city.
type Tour struct {
    City string
    Name string
    Time time.Time
}
```

Then you write the findTours function:

text/tours/fold/tours.go
```go
Line 1  // findTours returns all tours in city
   2    func findTours(db []*Tour, city string) []*Tour {
   3        var tours []*Tour
```

```
4     for _, t := range db {
5         if strings.EqualFold(t.City, city) {
6             tours = append(tours, t)
7         }
8     }
9     return tours
10  }
```

Finally, you test your code:

`text/tours/fold/tours.go`
```
// date is a shortcut to create time.Time from year, month, day
func date(year int, month time.Month, day int) time.Time {
    return time.Date(year, month, day, 0, 0, 0, 0, time.UTC)
}

func main() {
    db := []*Tour{
        {"Gdańsk", "Polish Food", date(2021, 1, 1)},
        {"Kraków", "Pub to Pub", date(2021, 1, 2)},
    }
    tours := findTours(db, "gdańsk")
    fmt.Printf("number of tours found: %d\n", len(tours))
}
```

When you run your code, you see this:

```
$ go run tours.go
number of tours found: 1
```

Discussion

On line 5, you use the strings.EqualFold function to compare cities.

You might be used to using strings.ToLower or strings.ToUpper for case-insensitive comparison. These functions will work well for case-insensitive comparisons when you work with English-only text.

Origin of Lower- and Uppercase

 The terms *lowercase* and *uppercase* come from the old days of the printing press. The physical letters were kept in cases. One of these cases was lower (closer to the compositor) and contained what we call "lowercase" letters. You can guess the name of the other case.

Other languages, however, are not as easy as English. For example, the Greek letter sigma has three forms: Σ at the start of a word, σ in the middle of the word, and ς at the end of a word. To help with these cases, the strings package provides EqualFold. EqualFold gets two strings and returns true if they match in a Unicode-aware case insensitivity.

A nice side effect of using EqualFold is that, unlike ToLower, it doesn't create another string just to check for equality. It'll work faster and with less memory consumption—a win/win.

If, for performance, you want to store strings already folded, you'll need to use the external golang.org/x/text/cases package. That package provides a Fold function that returns a Caser, which does Unicode-aware case folding.

Using Unicode Normalization for Comparison

Task

Your QA opens the following issues for you:

> In some cases, the search for cities returns lower-than-expected results. I can't exactly pin the issues, but it happens when non-English letters are involved.

You head over to the QA office and ask them to show you a failing example. After a search in their browser history—no funny stuff there—you come up with the following failing test:

```
text/tours/norm/tours_book.go
db := []*Tour{
    {"Gdańsk", "Polish Food", date(2021, 1, 1)},
    {"Kraków", "Pub to Pub", date(2021, 1, 2)},
}
tours := findTours(db, "Kraków")
fmt.Printf("number of tours found: %d\n", len(tours))
```

PDF and Unicode

 Due to Unicode issues in the PDF, the file shown here is tours_book.go; to see the actual problem in code, check out tours.go in the same directory.

When you run the code, you see the following output:

```
$ go run tours.go
number of tours found: 0
```

Now it's time to dig in ...

Solution

You start by looking at the length of the two similar cities:

```
text/tours/norm/tours_book.go
city1, city2 := "Kraków", "Kraków"
fmt.Println("city1:", len(city1))
fmt.Println("city2:", len(city2))
```

You receive this output:

```
city1: 7
city2: 8
```

You're getting warmer. You start reading about Unicode and get to the section about normalization forms. Now you have an idea how to fix the issues (more on normalization in the discussion).

You write a function that will Unicode-normalize a string:

```
text/tours/norm/tours.go
// normString normalizes string in NFKC format
func normString(s string) string {
    return norm.NFKC.String(s)
}
```

Then you add a NewTour function that will normalize the city name:

```
text/tours/norm/tours.go
// NewTour returns a new Tour.
func NewTour(city, name string, time time.Time) *Tour {
    tour := Tour{
        City: normString(city),
        Name: name,
        Time: time,
    }
    return &tour
}
```

Now you can use normString in your findTours function:

```
text/tours/norm/tours.go
Line 1  // findTours returns all tours in city
   -    func findTours(db []*Tour, city string) []*Tour {
   -        city = normString(city)
   -        var tours []*Tour
   5        for _, t := range db {
   -            if strings.EqualFold(t.City, city) {
   -                tours = append(tours, t)
   -            }
   -        }
```

```
10      return tours
   }
```

And then you try it out:

```
$ go run tours.go
number of tours found: 1
```

Discussion

Computers were first developed in English-speaking countries—the United Kingdom and the United States.

When early developers wanted to encode text in computers that understand only bits, they came out with the scheme known as ASCII,[3] which uses a byte (8 bits) to represent a character. To be precise, ASCII uses only 7 bits, and LATIN-1 extends it to 8 bits. For example, a is 97 (01100001), b is 98, and so on.

One byte is enough for the English alphabet, which contains twenty-six lowercase letters, twenty-six uppercase letters, and ten digits. Some space is even left for other special characters (for example, 9 for tab).

After a while, other countries started to use computers, and they wanted to write using their native languages.

ASCII wasn't good enough; a single byte isn't big enough to hold all the numbers we need to represent letters in different languages. This shortfall led to several different encoding schemes; the most common one is UTF-8.[4]

Did You Know?

 Rob Pike, one of the creators of Go, is also one of the creators of UTF-8.

The reason your code didn't find any tours is that the form in the database is normalized in NFC, whereas the search term in the query string is normalized in NFD.

To compare two strings, you need to normalize them. Currently, four normalization forms[5] are defined in the Unicode specification: NFC, NFD, NFKC, and NFKD.

---

3.   https://datatracker.ietf.org/doc/html/rfc20
4.   https://datatracker.ietf.org/doc/html/rfc3629
5.   https://unicode.org/reports/tr15/

The lesson here is always to normalize your string to a single form at the *edges* of your program and internally work with a single form.

The external packages under golang.org/x/text/ utilities work with Unicode.

Final Thoughts

Text is universal; it's used by many programs and, of course, by us humans. Working effectively with text in these modern days requires you to learn about Unicode. Go has excellent support for Unicode in the standard library as well as in external packages. I encourage you to keep what you saw here in mind, and if the need arises, dive deeper into the Unicode bottomless pool.

Next we'll look at one of the most basic constructs of programming—functions.

## CHAPTER 5

Working with Functions

Functions are the basic building blocks of your programs. Go's functions are first-class objects,[1] which means you can pass functions as arguments to other functions, create functions on the fly, and store functions in variables or data structures.

In this chapter, we're going to store functions in a map for flexibility, pass them as arguments to other functions, and create them on the fly for option handling.

Recipe 26

Using a Function Registry

Task

You're working with the operations team to help with the visibility of your website. Sophia, who leads the ops team, opens an issue for you:

> Currently our metrics server exposes metrics in JSON format. However, we'd like to expose metrics in different formats. Currently there's a demand for CSV and XML formats. But let's make it flexible so that adding new formats won't be a lot of work.

After a follow-up session that helps you understand the requirements and the formats better, you're ready to start coding. You decide to implement CSV first and once it's approved add XML.

---

1. https://dave.cheney.net/2016/11/13/do-not-fear-first-class-functions

---

Metric Database

In real production scenarios, you'll use an existing metrics database. Two most common ones (as of time of writing) are Prometheus[2] and InfluxDB.[3] They're both written in Go and are pretty awesome—you should check them out.

Solution

You start by defining an Encoder type, which is a function that encodes a slice of Metric into an io.Writer. We also define a registry from the desired output type (called mime type) to an Encoder function.

funcs/enc/enc.go

```go
var (
    // mime type → encoder function
    registry = make(map[string]Encoder)
)

// Encoder function
type Encoder func(w io.Writer, metrics []Metric) error
```

The Register function registers an encoder with a mime type.

funcs/enc/enc.go

```go
// Register registers an encoder for a mime type.
// It'll panic if format already registered.
func Register(mimeType string, enc Encoder) error {
    if _, ok := registry[mimeType]; ok {
        return fmt.Errorf("%q already registered", mimeType)
    }
    registry[mimeType] = enc
    return nil
}
```

Next, you define two encoders, a JSON encoder and a CSV encoder.

funcs/enc/enc.go

```go
// EncodeJSON encodes metrics in JSON format to w.
func EncodeJSON(w io.Writer, metrics []Metric) error {
    return json.NewEncoder(w).Encode(metrics)
}

// EncodeCSV encodes metrics in CSV format to w
func EncodeCSV(w io.Writer, metrics []Metric) error {
    wtr := csv.NewWriter(w)
```

---

2.   https://prometheus.io/

3.   https://www.influxdata.com/

```go
    // Write header
    if err := wtr.Write([]string{"time", "name", "value"}); err != nil {
        return err
    }
    // Record to write
    r := make([]string, 3)
    for _, s := range metrics {
        r[0] = s.Time.Format(time.RFC3339)
        r[1] = s.Name
        r[2] = fmt.Sprintf("%f", s.Value)
        if err := wtr.Write(r); err != nil {
            return err
        }
    }
    wtr.Flush()
    return nil
}
```

You register these two encoders in init.

funcs/enc/enc.go

```go
func init() {
    Register(csvMimeType, EncodeCSV)
    Register(jsonMimeType, EncodeJSON)
}
```

And now, you can use this infrastructure in our HTTP handler function.

funcs/enc/enc.go

```go
func queryHandler(w http.ResponseWriter, r *http.Request) {
    // Get query string from HTTP "query" parameter
    query := r.URL.Query().Get("query")
    if query == "" {
        http.Error(w, "missing query", http.StatusBadRequest)
        return
    }

    mimeType := requestMimeType(r)

    enc, ok := registry[mimeType]
    if !ok {
        msg := fmt.Sprintf("unsupported mime type - %q", mimeType)
        http.Error(w, msg, http.StatusBadRequest)
        return
    }

    metrics, err := queryDB(query)
    if err != nil {
        msg := fmt.Sprintf("can't query - %s", err)
        http.Error(w, msg, http.StatusBadRequest)
        return
    }
```

```
    w.Header().Add("Content-Type", mimeType)
    if err := enc(w, metrics); err != nil {
        size := len(metrics)
        const format = "can't encode %d metrics with %q - %s"
        log.Printf(format, size, mimeType, err)
    }
}

func requestMimeType(r *http.Request) string {
    // Get mime type from HTTP Accept header
    mimeType := r.Header.Get("Accept")
    if mimeType == "" || mimeType == "*/*" {
        return jsonMimeType // default to JSON
    }
    return mimeType
}
```

In main you mount our handler to the /metrics path and start the server.

funcs/enc/enc.go
```
func main() {
    http.HandleFunc("/metrics", queryHandler)
    addr := ":8080"
    log.Printf("server ready on %s", addr)
    if err := http.ListenAndServe(addr, nil); err != nil {
        log.Fatalf("error: %s", err)
    }
}
```

To test the server, you use the curl command-line HTTP client.

HTTP Clients

 If you don't like the command line, you can use visual tools such as Postman[4] or Insomnia.[5]

I use curl since I'm old and spend most of my time in the terminal.

You start the server and issue the following command:

```
$ curl 'http://localhost:8080/metrics?query=CPU'
# ...long JSON omitted...
```

By default, you get JSON.

---

4.   https://www.postman.com/
5.   https://insomnia.rest/

Now you can use the Accept HTTP header to request CSV.

```
$ curl -H 'Accept: text/csv' 'http://localhost:8080/metrics?query=CPU'
time,name,value
2020-05-31T17:29:04+03:00,CPU,60.466029
2020-05-31T17:28:04+03:00,CPU,94.050909
2020-05-31T17:27:04+03:00,CPU,66.456005
2020-05-31T17:26:04+03:00,CPU,43.771419
2020-05-31T17:25:04+03:00,CPU,42.463750
2020-05-31T17:24:04+03:00,CPU,68.682307
2020-05-31T17:23:04+03:00,CPU,6.563702
```

Discussion

The registry map allows you to add more encoders without changing the code inside queryHandler. You can use this registry method (sometimes called *dispatch*) since functions are first-class objects in Go and can be stored in other data structures—a map in our case.

The client for our web server will use the Accept HTTP header to specify the desired output format from our server. If the HTTP Accept header is not provided, you emit JSON back to the client.

Make sure to set the Content-Type HTTP header before sending data back to the client. This header information will allow the client to know what type of data (like JSON or CSV) it's getting back.

The most known use of a function registry is a web server router (also known as a "mux," which is short for "multiplexer"). Every time you write code like http.HandleFunc("/api/health", healthHandler), the router registers the healthHandler function to be called when someone accesses /api/health.

Another example of this registry pattern is database/sql in the standard library, which provides the interfaces to work with a relational database and a registry mechanism. database/sql does not supply any specific database driver.

If you want to work with a specific database (for example, SQLite[6]), you'll need to import the external package for it; the package will register itself as a database driver for this specific type. Since you're importing the database driver package just for the side effect of the registration, you need to do an _ (underscore) import.

---

6. https://www.sqlite.org/index.html

Here's an example:

```go
package main

import (
        "database/sql"
        "log"

        // Using sqlite3, this will register "sqlite3" protocol
        _ "github.com/mattn/go-sqlite3"
)

func main() {
        db, err := sql.Open("sqlite3", "metrics.db")
        if err != nil {
                log.Fatalf("error: %s", err)
        }
        defer db.Close()
        // Start using db

}
```

Recipe 27

Using Functions as Options

Task

Alex, who wrote a popular server library that is used by several teams, decided to take a year off and sail in the Pacific. After some discussions, your boss, Jessie, assigns you to maintain the library. In the kickoff meeting she says:

> Please go over all the open issues we have for the library. Try to find common issues and assign priorities to them.

After spending some quality time with the bug tracker, you see a lot of requests to add new options to the server: which port to listen, log verbosity, and more.

Jessie agrees that this is a good place to start and adds:

> Please try to keep the API as-is, I don't want anyone to change their code every time we add an option.

Solution

The code defines a Server struct.

funcs/server/server.go
```
// Server is an HTTP server.
type Server struct {
    verbose bool
    port    int
}
```

You add a variable number of options to the NewServer function:

funcs/server/server.go
```
// NewServer returns a Server with options.
func NewServer(options ...func(*Server) error) (*Server, error) {
    srv := &Server{
        port: 8080, // default port
    }
    for _, opt := range options {
        if err := opt(srv); err != nil {
            return nil, err
        }
    }

    return srv, nil
}
```

An option is a function that gets a *Server as a parameter and returns an error value.

You first create a new *Server struct, called srv, with default values. Then you apply each of the parameters to srv, allowing them to change the configuration values.

Now you define your first option:

funcs/server/server.go
```
// WithVerbose sets the verbose option on s.
func WithVerbose(s *Server) error {
    s.verbose = true
    return nil
}
```

Discussion

Ellipsis (...) is Go's way of writing a variable number of arguments.

Inside NewServer options is a slice of func(*Server) error. By passing a variable number of arguments to NewServer, we allow the user to pass zero or more options. If the user doesn't pass any options, the server will be created with default values.

Making the Server struct configuration-related fields unexported gives you the freedom to change the implementation of Server (for example, renaming verbose to noisy) without users being aware.

This recipe is a practical example of using a function as an argument to another function.

Functional Options

 This recipe is a variation on Dave Cheney's "Functional options for friendly APIs." See Dave Cheney's website[7] for more information.

Recipe 28

Using Closures to Provide Options with Arguments

Task

Jessie agrees that options as functions are a good idea. She says:

> This looks good, but I'd like to also see an example of an option that takes an argument.

You decide to start with a WithPort(port) option that will configure the port the server listens on, in case there are collisions in the port number.

Solution

You define WithPort for configuration of that port:

```
funcs/server/server.go
const portErrFmt = "port must be between 0 and %d, got %d"

func WithPort(port int) func(*Server) error {
    const maxPort = 0xFFFF
    return func(s *Server) error {
        if port <= 0 || port > maxPort {
            return fmt.Errorf(portErrFmt, maxPort, port)
        }
```

---

7. https://dave.cheney.net/2014/10/17/functional-options-for-friendly-apis

```
        s.port = port
        return nil
    }
}
```

Discussion

WithPort is a function that gets a port argument and returns a server option function.

The func keyword is used to create functions; in most cases you'll define function with func and then a name:

```
func Add(a, b int) int {
        return a + b
}
```

However, you can write the same code in a different way:

```
var Add = func(a, b int) int {
        return a + b
}
```

You use this syntax in WithPort; since you don't name the function we create, it's called an *anonymous function*.

This anonymous function remembers port from its closure. In short, a function closure is the environment where it was defined. Every function has a closure; when the Go compiler looks for for variables (such as port), it will search the function closure as well.

The concept of closure[8] is not unique to Go—most programming languages have it.

Function arguments are evaluated before being passed to the function. Say you use the following:

```
srv, err := NewServer(WithPort(9999))
```

WithPort(9999) is evaluated first, and its return value matches the type of arguments that NewServer consumes.

---

8. https://go.dev/tour/moretypes/25

Recipe 29

Passing Notifications with Functions

Task

You're working on a new system that will execute tasks for the company's data pipeline. Your boss asks you to come up with a generic way to handle various tasks and also a way to notify watchers when a task is done. After some thinking and experimenting, you decide to use functions for task execution and notification.

Solution

You start by writing a Task struct that will have the work to run as a function and also a slice of functions for notification:

```
funcs/task/task.go
// State is task state.
type State byte

const (
    Ready State = iota + 1
    Working
    Done
)

// Task is a task to execute.
type Task struct {
    ID      uint
    Result any
    Err     error
    State   State

    Work     func() (any, error)
    Watchers []func(*Task)
}

// NewTask returns a new Task that will execute work.
func NewTask(id uint, work func() (any, error)) *Task {
    t := Task{
        ID:    id,
        State: Ready,
        Work:  work,
    }
    return &t
}
```

Then write a Subscribe method that allows watchers to subscribe to notifications:

funcs/task/task.go
```
// Subscribe subscribes a watcher to task.
func (t *Task) Subscribe(w func(*Task)) {
    t.Watchers = append(t.Watchers, w)
}
```

Next, you write the Execute method that will run the work, update the task state, and notify:

funcs/task/task.go
```
Line 1  // Execute executes the task.
-       func (t *Task) Execute() error {
-           t.State = Working
-           defer func() { t.State = Done }()
5
-           t.Result, t.Err = t.Work()
-           if t.Err != nil {
-               log.Printf("error: Task %d failed - %s", t.ID, t.Err)
-           }
10
-           // Notify watchers
-           for _, s := range t.Watchers {
-               s(t)
-           }
15
-           return t.Err
-       }
```

Then, to test the code, you write a Watcher:

funcs/task/task.go
```
// Watcher is a task watcher.
type Watcher struct{}

func (w *Watcher) Handle(t *Task) {
    log.Printf("info: w2: from %d - %#v %v", t.ID, t.Result, t.Err)
}
```

And finally, you write some code to try the system:

funcs/task/task.go
```
Line 1  t := NewTask(7, func() (any, error) { return "done", nil })
2       t.Subscribe(func(t *Task) {
3           log.Printf("info: w1: from %d - %#v %v", t.ID, t.Result, t.Err)
4       })
5       var w Watcher
6       t.Subscribe(w.Handle)
7
8       t.Execute()
```

When you run the code, you see the following output:

```
2023/06/21 16:17:52 info: w1: from 7 - "done" <nil>
2023/06/21 16:17:52 info: w2: from 7 - "done" <nil>
```

Discussion

The Work field is a function without argument that returns any and an error. You can probably make this code more type-safe by using generics, but for the sake of simplicity we'll keep it any. Head over to Recipe 39, Using Generics to Reduce Code Size, on page 111, to see generics recipes. This function represents the work the task should do. The return values from this function are stored in the Result and Err fields.

In line 4, you use defer to make sure that when Execute exits, the status is Done even if there's any early exit or a panic.

The Watchers field is a slice of function that takes a *Task as an argument. Once the task finishes running Work, it'll call each function in Watcher with itself. The watchers have access to all the information from the task and can do what they want with it.

In line 6, we pass a *bound method* as a function. This makes Subscribe flexible—both functions and methods can be passed as watchers.

Recipe 30

Accessing Unexported Functions

Task

You're working on a new image-processing stage in the data pipeline. The company has a ready-made client to fetch data from the central data lake.

However, the client has a 1 MB limit on message body size. But some of the images are up to 4.2 MB. You dig through the client code and see an unexported function:

funcs/files/client/client.go
```
func setMaxBodySize(size int64) int64 {
```

You start a chat with Mae, the client lead developer:

[You]
Hi. I'm using your client, and it has a 1 MB limit on body size. I need to
make it bigger and saw you have an unexported `setMaxBodySize` function.
Any chance you can make it exported?

[Mae]
Hi. Thanks for using my client.
I need to think about this. There are many users to the client library, and
we have strict performance considerations.
Also, I'm pretty busy this quarter, so the fastest I can get to this is in
two months---sorry. But go ahead and open an issue so I won't forget.

[You]
I understand, thanks. I'll open an issue.

Your deadline is much shorter than two months. You open issue #732 and
start looking for other solutions.

Solution

You decide to use the go:linkname compiler directive.

funcs/files/files.go
```
import (
    "fmt"
    _ "unsafe"

    "git.corp.com/client"
)

// HACK: Access internal client.setMaxBodySize.
// Remove this once setMaxBodySize becomes exported, see issue #732.

//go:linkname setClientMaxBodySize git.corp.com/client.setMaxBodySize
func setClientMaxBodySize(int64)
```

Now you can use setClientMaxBodySize in your code.

funcs/files/files.go
```
setClientMaxBodySize(5 * 1_000_000) // 5 MB
c := client.New()
// Start using client with big images...
```

Discussion

Go has several compiler directives (sometimes known as *pragmas*). The
directives are comments that start with prefix //go:. These directives change
how the compiler treats the current file or a piece of code below the comment.
For example, the //go:build directive affects when the current file will be built.
See *Using Build Tags for Conditional Builds* on how to use it.

The go:linkname comment is one of Go's compiler directives.

The documentation of go:linkname says:

> This directive determines the object-file symbol used for a Go var or func declaration, allowing two Go symbols to alias the same object-file symbol, thereby enabling one package to access a symbol in another package even when this would violate the usual encapsulation of unexported declarations, or even type safety.

You can do many dirty tricks with go:linkname, but you shouldn't without a very good reason. Dirty tricks get the job done, but there's always a cost to pay—the code is less readable, it's hard to understand which function is actually getting called, and unexported functions can change without notice.

The Go developers force you to import the unsafe package when using go:linkname so it'll be in your mind. In the code, you also wrote a comment to that effect. It might be a good idea to open an issue to remove this hack so you won't forget, just like you do with any other technical debt.

You might take some other approaches instead of using go:linkname:

Vendoring

You can run go mod vendor, and then the client code will be locally in the vendor directory. Then you can fix the code in the vendor directory. However, you'll need to manually add fixes to the client library on every change. Also, the vendor directory tends to get pretty big, and updates to it have very big diffs.

Replace

You can use a replace directive in the go.mod file and have the client file locally. This approach complicates the build process and has the same issue with updates as vendoring.

Fork

You can fork the client code to another repository. It has the same issues as in vendoring.

You can access more than unexported functions using go:linkname. See the "Accessing Private Functions, Methods, Types and Variables in Go"[9] post by Yarden Laifenfeld for examples.

To access more compiler directives you can use, see the compiler command documentation[10] or "Go's hidden #pragmas"[11] by Dave Cheney. For example,

---

I sometimes use go:noinline in my benchmarks to make sure the benchmarked code is not inlined by the compiler.

Final Thoughts

With creative thinking, you can use this ability to write compact solutions, as we saw in the metrics database and options recipes.

We also saw that using first-class functions isn't that esoteric; even the built-in database/sql package uses them.

Now go and look at your code—are there any places you can use functions as first-class objects to simplify it?

Next, we'll take a look at some of Go's built-in types and see how you can use them in your code.

## CHAPTER 6

Working with Basic Types

As a modern language, Go provides several built-in types that are useful in various scenarios. Some of these types are:

- Numbers
- Strings
- Slices (called lists or arrays in other languages)
- Maps
- Time (also known as timestamp)

For each of these types, the Go developers had to make some design decisions that affect how these types behave. In this chapter, we'll look at the typical use cases for each type and consider the design decisions the Go developers made while developing them.

All of these types might seem simple, but each has its own unique characteristics. If you don't understand how these types work, you'll find yourself looking at some interesting bugs and performance issues.

Of the basic types, time can be the most challenging. Time might seem like a simple concept—you book a restaurant table for 7 p.m. and don't think about it much. Under the hood, the computer doing the reservation has many issues to worry about: time zones, daylight saving time, leap year, leap seconds, and more.

Go's time.Time package provides most of the functionality you'll need to work with times and durations.

Recipe 31

Using the comma, ok Paradigm

Task

You're working on an online store that sells fresh fruits and vegetables from local farmers. This morning you see that Frank, the QA, has assigned a bug to you. Frank has a knack for finding interesting bugs, and you're always happy to solve the puzzles he comes up with. The issue says:

> For some reason, when we apply discount to a shopping cart, the price comes out wrong. See the test that follows.

types/discount/discount_test.go
```go
func Test_cartTotal(t *testing.T) {
    cart := []LineItem{
        {"lemon", 4, 0.5},
        {"orange", 5, 0.4},
        {"banana", 6, 0.1},
    }
    discounts := map[string]float64{
        "orange": 0.9, // 10% discount on oranges
    }
    expected := 4*0.5 + 5*0.4*0.9 + 6*0.1
    total := cartTotal(cart, discounts)
    require.InDelta(t, expected, total, 0.001)
}
```

The cart total should come out to 4.4, but this code prints 1.8.

You start by reacquainting yourself with the code. You look at LineItem:

types/discount/discount.go
```go
// LineItem is an item in a shopping cart.
type LineItem struct {
    Name   string
    Amount float64 // units or weight in pounds
    Price  float64
}
```

And then you check cartTotal, which works with discounts:

types/discount/discount.go
```go
// cartTotal calculates total price of cart after applying discounts.
// discounts is a map from Name -> discount value.
func cartTotal(cart []LineItem, discounts map[string]float64) float64 {
    total := 0.0
    for _, li := range cart {
        discount := discounts[li.Name]
        total += li.Amount * li.Price * discount
    }
    return total
}
```

Now it's time to think and squash some bugs.

Solution

Looking at the code, you see that there's only a discount to orange, but the cart also has lemon and banana. Going over the Go documentation, you see that a map will return zero value for non-existing keys. In the discounts cases, the values are float64, so the zero value will be 0.0. Which means after discount, the prices of lemon and banana will be 0.

You write the following code to fix cartTotal:

types/discount/fix/discount.go
```go
// cartTotal calculates total price of cart after applying discounts.
// discounts is a map from Name -> discount value.
func cartTotal(cart []LineItem, discounts map[string]float64) float64 {
    total := 0.0
    for _, li := range cart {
        discount, ok := discounts[li.Name]
        if ok {
            total += li.Amount * li.Price * discount
        } else {
            total += li.Amount * li.Price
        }
    }
    return total
}
```

Running the code now, it prints 4.4 as expected.

Discussion

The design decision to return zero value for non-existing keys makes your code more predictable. However, this poses an issue: how do you know whether you got a zero value because the key is missing or because it's actually the value set in the map?

The solution in Go is to use the comma, ok paradigm.

When you write value, ok := m[key] for some map m, ok is a Boolean value and will be true if your key is in the map and false otherwise.

Apart from maps, there are two other cases where you can use the comma, ok paradigm.

This zero versus missing problem appears in two more places in Go—channels and type assertion.

The first case is receiving from a channel. When you receive from a closed channel, you'll get the zero value:

```
types/other/other.go
ch := make(chan int)
close(ch)

val, ok := <-ch
fmt.Println("val =", val, "ok =", ok)
```

The second case is type assertion (for example, val.(int)). By default, if a type assertion fails, it will panic.

You can use comma, ok here as well:

```
types/other/other.go
var i any = "hi"
// n := i.(int) will panic
if n, ok := i.(int); ok {
    fmt.Println("int", n)
} else {
    fmt.Println("not an int")
}
```

Remember the comma, ok paradigm—it will simplify your code and protect you from bugs or panics due to zero values. It's also the only way to tell if a zero value you got is from user input or due to missing data.

Using a Slice to Implement a Stack

Task

You're working on a fancy new editor that will make developers at least ten times more productive. Jane, your team lead, asks you to work on highlighting matching parentheses. Every time the user enters a closing parenthesis, say, ')' or '}', you need to highlight the matching opening parenthesis.

After some thinking, you decide to use a stack of opening parentheses. Once the user enters a closing parenthesis, you check if it matches the top of the stack. If so, you pop from the stack and highlight the matching opening parenthesis.

Solution

You start by defining a Token struct that holds the opening parenthesis and its location:

```
types/slices/stack/stack.go
type Token struct {
    Loc  int
    Char rune
}
```

Next, you define a Stack type and give it a Len method:

```
types/slices/stack/stack.go
// Stack is a stack of tokens
type Stack []Token

// Len returns the number of elements in the stack
func (s Stack) Len() int {
    return len(s)
}
```

Then you add the Push method:

```
types/slices/stack/stack.go
// Push pushes a value to the stack
func (s *Stack) Push(tok Token) {
    *s = append(*s, tok)
}
```

And lastly, Pop (and ErrEmpty), which is the most complicated:

types/slices/stack/stack.go

```
Line 1  var (
     -      ErrEmpty = errors.New("empty stack")
     -  )

     5  // Pop pops an element from the stack
     -  func (s *Stack) Pop() (Token, error) {
     -      size := s.Len()

     -      if size == 0 {
    10          return Token{}, ErrEmpty
     -      }

     -      sl := *s // so we won't have to use (*s) everywhere
     -      val := sl[size-1]
    15      sl = sl[:size-1]

     -      // if we shrank by more than half and larger than 1k, free memory
     -      if len(sl) > 1024 && 2*len(sl) < cap(sl) {
     -          sl2 := make([]Token, len(sl))
    20          copy(sl2, sl)
     -          sl = sl2
     -      }

     -      *s = sl
    25      return val, nil
     -  }
```

Then you write some code to test your implementation:

types/slices/stack/stack.go

```
var s Stack
fmt.Println(s)
s.Push(Token{19, '('})
s.Push(Token{49, '['})
fmt.Println(s)
if v, err := s.Pop(); err != nil {
    fmt.Println("error", err)
} else {
    fmt.Println("pop", v)
}
```

When you run the code, you see the expected output:

```
[]
[{19 40} {49 91}]
pop {49 91}
```

Discussion

If you look at src/runtime/slice.go in the Go source code, you'll see the following definition:

```
type slice struct {
    array unsafe.Pointer
    len    int
    cap    int
}
```

A slice is a struct with three fields:

array
    A pointer to the underlying array in memory

len
    Number of elements in the slice

cap
    Number of elements from array to the end of the underlying array

Let's look at an example. You'll create an []int with five elements.

```
s1 := make([]int, 5)
```

The following image shows how it looks in memory:

Now define s2 to be a part of s1 by using slice notation:

```
s2 := s1[1:3]
```

Slice notation is half-open, meaning you get the first index (1) up to but not including the last (3). In this example, you get indices 1 and 2.

Now the memory looks like the following image:

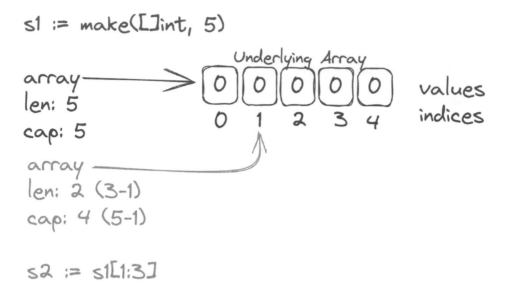

The Push implementation is using the built-in append function to add items to the stack. append might allocate a new underlying array and will return a slice, which might be a new one or a copy of the old one.

You use a pointer receiver in Pop and Push since you need to update the original slice with the value returned by append.

In Pop line 18, you check that the length (len) of s is less than half of the capacity (cap). If the condition is true, you create a new slice in size len, copy over the data, and then assign s to the new slice.

You do this check to avoid memory leaks. A Go object will stay in memory as long as there's a variable pointing to it, even indirectly. Since the array field in s points to the underlying array, the garbage collector won't free the underlying array even if s points to a small part of it.

Stacks are also used in parsers, virtual machines, and many other algorithms.

Calculating Cumulative Sum

Task

Josh, the ops team lead, asks you to help them with monitoring the server you are developing. He says:

> We have a cumSum function that calculates the cumulative sum of a slice of metrics. For example, the cumulative sum of []int{1, 2, 3} is []int{1, 3, 6}. When we use the function, we see that it gets slow on large slices, and the garbage collector starts to work a lot. Can you please have a look and fix it?

You look at the current code to calculate the cumulative sum:

types/slices/cumsum/cumsum.go
```go
// cumSum returns the cumulative sum of values
// cumSum([]int{1, 2, 3}) → []int{1, 3, 6}
func cumSum(values []int) []int {
    var cs []int
    s := 0
    for _, val := range values {
        s += val
        cs = append(cs, s)
    }
    return cs
}
```

Solution

Nothing jumps out as suspicious in the code, so you write a benchmark.

First, you initialize a values array in the init function so that our benchmark time will not include the time this initialization step takes:

types/slices/cumsum/bench_test.go
```go
var (
    values   []int
    size     = 9323
    expected int
)

func init() {
    for i := 0; i < size; i++ {
        values = append(values, i+1)
    }
```

```
    // sum of odd numbered arithmetic series
    expected = size * ((values[0] + values[size-1]) / 2)
}
```

And then you write the benchmark code:

types/slices/cumsum/bench_test.go
```
func BenchmarkCumsum(b *testing.B) {
    for i := 0; i < b.N; i++ {
        out := cumSum(values) // values is populated in init
        // Make sure compiler doesn't optimize the above call away
        if len(out) != len(values) {
            b.Fatalf("bad out length: %d", len(out))
        }
    }
}
```

Now you can run the benchmark, with memory information:

```
goos: linux
goarch: amd64
pkg: github.com/353solutions/go-cookbook/types/slices/cumsum
cpu: 12th Gen Intel(R) Core(TM) i7-1255U
BenchmarkCumsum-12    13896    87945 ns/op    357626 B/op    19 allocs/op
PASS
ok      github.com/353solutions/go-cookbook/types/slices/cumsum 2.102s
```

Running Benchmarks

 When you run this code on your machine, you'll see different numbers. You must run benchmarks on hardware as close as possible to production and on data that is close to the real data. Otherwise, you are lying to yourself.

An int on my machine is an alias to int64, which is 8 bytes. The size of values is 9323, so the memory usage should be around 8 * 9323 = 74,584. The size reported by the benchmark, 3,862,96, is much higher, and there are twenty allocations per operation. Why?

You decide to look at the profiling information:

```
$ go test -bench . -cpuprofile cpu.pprof
goos: linux
goarch: amd64
pkg: github.com/353solutions/go-cookbook/types/slices/cumsum
cpu: 12th Gen Intel(R) Core(TM) i7-1255U
BenchmarkCumsum-12        10000            113170 ns/op
PASS
ok      github.com/353solutions/go-cookbook/types/slices/cumsum 1.312s
```

```
$ go tool pprof cpu.pprof
File: cumsum.test
Type: cpu
Time: Jul 30, 2023 at 5:43pm (IDT)
Duration: 1.30s, Total samples = 2.22s (170.38%)
Entering interactive mode (type "help" for commands, "o" for options)
(pprof) top 10 -cum
Showing nodes accounting for 0.63s, 28.38% of 2.22s total
Dropped 50 nodes (cum <= 0.01s)
Showing top 10 nodes out of 131
      flat  flat%   sum%        cum   cum%
     0.03s  1.35%  1.35%      1.09s 49.10%  .../slices/cumsum.BenchmarkCumsum
         0     0%  1.35%      1.09s 49.10%  testing.(*B).launch
         0     0%  1.35%      1.09s 49.10%  testing.(*B).runN
         0     0%  1.35%      1.07s 48.20%  runtime.systemstack
     0.15s  6.76%  8.11%      1.06s 47.75%  .../slices/cumsum.cumSum (inline)
     0.01s  0.45%  8.56%      0.91s 40.99%  runtime.growslice
     0.01s  0.45%  9.01%      0.69s 31.08%  runtime.gcBgMarkWorker
         0     0%  9.01%      0.60s 27.03%  runtime.gcBgMarkWorker.func2
     0.02s   0.9%  9.91%      0.60s 27.03%  runtime.gcDrain
     0.41s 18.47% 28.38%      0.41s 18.47%  runtime.memmove
```

You see that slice-related functions, such as runtime.growslice take a big portion of the time. You look into how append works, and then you write your fix:

types/slices/cumsum/fix/cumsum.go
```go
// cumSum returns the cumulative sum of values
// cumSum([]int{1, 2, 3}) → []int{1, 3, 6}
func cumSum(values []int) []int {
➤    cs := make([]int, 0, len(values))
    s := 0
    for _, val := range values {
        s += val
        cs = append(cs, s)
    }
    return cs
}
```

To verify, you run the benchmark again:

```
$ go test -bench . -benchmem
goos: linux
goarch: amd64
pkg: github.com/353solutions/go-cookbook/types/slices/cumsum/fix
cpu: 12th Gen Intel(R) Core(TM) i7-1255U
BenchmarkCumsum-12     50569     23712 ns/op     81920 B/op     1 allocs/op
PASS
ok      github.com/353solutions/go-cookbook/types/slices/cumsum/fix     1.445s
```

It's much faster, with only a single memory allocation per operation.

Discussion

Starting with an empty slice and using append saves you from using indices, which are error prone.

Off-by-One Errors

One type of index error is *off-by-one*, in which a program iterates through a loop one too many or one too few times.

Read more about off-by-one errors at http://www.catb.org/jargon/html/O/off-by-one-error.html.

We pay a price for the append approach, however.

Every time you call append, it needs to check if there's enough space in the underlying array (cap) for the new element. If the underlying array is full, append will create a new array with a bigger size, copy over the old array, and append the new element.

Let's see that process in action. You're going to call append many times and report every time the underlying array capacity has changed:

```
types/slices/append_size/append_size.go
func main() {
    currCap := 0
    var s []int
    for i := 0; i < 2000; i++ {
        s = append(s, i)
        if c := cap(s); c != currCap {
            ratio := float64(c) / float64(currCap)
            fmt.Printf("%4d → %4d (%.2f)\n", currCap, c, ratio)
            currCap = c
        }
    }
}
```

And run it:

```
  0 →     1 (+Inf)
  1 →     2 (2.00)
  2 →     4 (2.00)
  4 →     8 (2.00)
  8 →    16 (2.00)
 16 →    32 (2.00)
 32 →    64 (2.00)
 64 →   128 (2.00)
128 →   256 (2.00)
256 →   512 (2.00)
```

```
 512 → 1024 (2.00)
1024 → 1280 (1.25)
1280 → 1696 (1.32)
1696 → 2304 (1.36)
```

You can see that up to 1024, append will double the size of the underlying array, and after that it'll grow the underlying array by about a third. Note that this growth policy might change between Go versions, but the general behavior will stay the same.

This growth means that in the original cumSum, append is allocating a lot of intermediate arrays, which causes memory bloat. Redundant allocations also cost in performance. It takes time to allocate data, and when the garbage collector runs, it has more garbage to clean.

You use the second form of the built-in make function, providing both length and capacity. In this case, you use 0 length to start with an empty slice and to ensure the underlying array has enough capacity.

Recipe 34

Serializing Time to/from JSON

Task

You are maintaining the operations team log system. Luna, your team lead, assigns you the following issue:

> We'd like to expose a REST API on top of the logging system so clients will be able to send log messages over HTTP in JSON format. Also, clients should be able to query the server and get log records as JSON. Oh, and due to some legacy systems, the time format used should be YYYYMMDDTHHMMSS.MS (for example, 20230421T153217.372).

You dig through the code and find the definition of a Log struct:

```
types/time/json/json.go
// LogRecord is a log record.
type LogRecord struct {
    Time     time.Time
    Level    string
    Message  string
}
```

Now it's time to code.

Solution

You start by defining a JSONTime struct that will serialize to/from JSON in the requested format:

types/time/json/json.go

```go
// JSONTimeLayout is time format in JSON.
const JSONTimeLayout = "20060102T150405.000"

// JSONTime is a time with different JSON encoding format.
type JSONTime struct {
    time.Time
}

// MarshalJSON implements json.Marshaler
func (t JSONTime) MarshalJSON() ([]byte, error) {
    s := t.Format(JSONTimeLayout)
    return []byte(`"` + s + `"`), nil
}

// UnmarshalJSON implements json.Unmarshaler
func (t *JSONTime) UnmarshalJSON(data []byte) error {
    // Example input: "20230727T170756.246"
    if len(data) < 2 {
        return fmt.Errorf("data too small: %q", string(data))
    }

    data = data[1 : len(data)-1] // trim enclosing ""
    ts, err := time.Parse(JSONTimeLayout, string(data))
    if err != nil {
        return err
    }

    t.Time = ts
    return nil
}
```

Then you define APILogRecord, which will be used in the API layer and a couple of conversion functions:

types/time/json/json.go

```go
// APILogRecord is a log record used in the API.
type APILogRecord struct {
    Time    JSONTime `json:"time"`
    Level   string   `json:"level"`
    Message string   `json:"message"`
}
```

```go
// APItoLog converts APILogRecord to LogRecord.
func APItoLog(r APILogRecord) LogRecord {
    lr := LogRecord{
        Time:    r.Time.Time,
        Level:   r.Level,
        Message: r.Message,
    }
    return lr
}

// LogtoAPI converts LogRecord to APILogRecord.
func LogtoAPI(r LogRecord) APILogRecord {
    ar := APILogRecord{
        Time: JSONTime{r.Time},
        Level: r.Level, Message: r.Message,
    }
    return ar
}
```

And finally, you write a bit of code to test:

types/time/json/json.go

```go
r := APILogRecord{
    Time:    JSONTime{time.Unix(1585318985, 79993962)},
    Level:   "INFO",
    Message: "something happened",
}
data, err := json.Marshal(r)
if err != nil {
    log.Fatalf("error: %s", err)
}
fmt.Println(string(data))

var r2 APILogRecord
if err := json.Unmarshal(data, &r2); err != nil {
    log.Fatalf("error: %s", err)
}
fmt.Printf("%+v\n", r2)
```

You get this output:

```
{"time":"20200327T172305.079","level":"INFO","message":"something happened"}
{Time:2020-03-27 17:23:05.079 +0000 UTC Level:INFO Message:something happened}
```

Discussion

The JSON[1] format does not have a Time data type.

Two common solutions are used for serializing time data to JSON:

- Convert the time to a number (usually seconds since epoch)
- Convert the time to a string (for example, 2020-03-27T17:17:37+03:00)

The second option makes it easier for us humans to understand the time value encoded in the JSON message (consider "2022-05-08T11:39:06.300097479Z" versus 1652009946).

The built-in encoding/json package uses this approach. It encodes time.Time to a JSON string in RFC3339[2] format. It would have been great if everyone else used the same format. But as you know, getting two software engineers to agree on one thing is hard, let alone all of them. See XKCD 927[3] if you need more proof.

You implement json.Marshaler and json.Unmarshaler interfaces to support custom time format in JSONTime. To decouple this API-specific implementation from the LogRecord used internally, you create APILogRecord. This way, if someone changes LogRecord, it won't affect the API.

To get easy access to the built-in time (and time methods), you embed time.Time inside JSONTime.

Recipe 35

Using Composite Keys in Maps

Task

As a hobby, you work on some algorithmic trading code. After a gaming night with your friend Bob, who works in a bank, you decide you need a fast in-memory database for the stock information. You're going to use this database to train stock-trading algorithms that will make you rich!

---

1. https://www.json.org/json-en.html
2. https://datatracker.ietf.org/doc/html/rfc3339
3. https://xkcd.com/927/

Stock Trading

This is in no way a recommendation to trade the stock market. I worked for several years in high-frequency trading companies, and the volume of information we had gave us a huge advantage over casual traders.

Automated trading is very risky—the Knight Capital Group lost $440 million in forty-five minutes due to a bug. Do you think you can stand such losses?

Solution

The information for a stock is the opening, low, high, and closing price of the day (known as OHLC).

```
types/stock_db/stock_db.go
// StockInfo is information about stock at a given date.
type StockInfo struct {
    Date    time.Time
    Symbol  string
    Open    float64
    High    float64
    Low     float64
    Close   float64
}
```

You want fast access for stock information at a given date, and you decide to use a map and have a struct as a composite key. This is the key:

```
types/stock_db/stock_db.go
type key struct {
    year    int
    month   time.Month
    day     int
    symbol  string
}
```

Then you write an InfoDB struct that will hold the map:

```
types/stock_db/stock_db.go
// InfoDB is in memory stock database.
type InfoDB struct {
    m map[key]StockInfo
}
```

InfoDB provides a Get function that will return stock information for given stock at a given date:

types/stock_db/stock_db.go
```go
// Get return information for stock at date. If information is not found the
// second return value will be false.
func (i *InfoDB) Get(symbol string, date time.Time) (StockInfo, bool) {
    k := key{date.Year(), date.Month(), date.Day(), symbol}
    info, ok := i.m[k]
    return info, ok
}
```

Discussion

Most of the time, map keys will be a simple type, but in some cases, you'll need a composite key. A composite key is a key that consists of two or more attributes.

I've seen people who, instead of using composite keys, create a string that represents the composite key. For example, for our database case you might construct a string key with values such as "AAPL:20200302". This approach is error prone; you're inventing a new serialization format and might create the same string for two different keys.

For example, assume that a user is defined by its login name and a user ID. If you create the string "joe42", it might be user joe with user ID 42 or the user joe4 with the ID 2.

We're taking advantage of the fact that a Go struct is comparable if all of its fields are comparable. You can use these structs as map keys without figuring out a bulletproof way of creating strings to represent keys.

Some types, such as slices, are not comparable and can't be used in composite keys. If you need to use a slice as a map key, or a part of a map key, convert it to a string first. However, since a user might change the original slice, it's better not to use slices as map keys at all.

In general, prefer types that can't be changed (immutable), such as string, int, or rune, as map keys.

You decided not to use time.Time as part of the compound key since comparing with time.Time can be tricky. See Recipe 36, Parsing Time Strings, on page 99, for more information.

Recipe 36

Parsing Time Strings

Task

You're working in a news agency, helping with data storage. Phil, the product manager, assigns an issue for you:

> We'd like to help journalists search for articles in a specific time. The journalists aren't that tech savvy, so we'd like to support more natural language in the queries. Here are some examples:
>
> - 2 weeks ago
> - today
> - 5 hours ago
> - 2020-03-02T11:47
>
> Since we have customers from all over the world, we need to support time zones as well. The time zone will be in [] at the end of the query—for example, today [Australia/Sydney]. If time zone is not specified, use UTC.

You start by going over the documentation of the time package and then start to code.

Solution

You start by looking at time zones. You decide to use a regular expression to find the time zone specification in the query string and parse it.

```
types/time/parse_time/parse_time.go
var tzRe = regexp.MustCompile(`\[.+\]`)

// extractLocation will extract location information from query (e.g.
// "today [US/Pacific]". It returns the location and trimmed query
// (without location)
func extractLocation(query string) (*time.Location, string, error) {
    loc := tzRe.FindStringIndex(query)
    if loc == nil { // No time zone in query, return UTC
        return time.UTC, query, nil
    }

    // ±1 to remove []
    locName := query[loc[0]+1 : loc[1]-1]
    tz, err := time.LoadLocation(locName)
    if err != nil {
        return nil, query, err
    }
```

```
    // Remove time zone from query
    query = strings.TrimSpace(query[:loc[0]])
    return tz, query, nil
}
```

Next you move to today:

types/time/parse_time/parse_time.go

```
func today(loc *time.Location) time.Time {
    t := time.Now().In(loc)
    t = time.Date(t.Year(), t.Month(), t.Day(), 0, 0, 0, 0, t.Location())
    return t
}
```

Then you write parseDelta, which will parse a time delta:

types/time/parse_time/parse_time.go

```
var unitNames = map[string]time.Duration{
    "minute": time.Minute,
    "hour":   time.Hour,
    "day":    24 * time.Hour,
    "week":   7 * 24 * time.Hour,
}

// parseDelta parses a string like "3 days" and returns time.Duration
// (3 * 24 * time.Hour) and the rounding duration (24 * time.Hour)
func parseDelta(query string) (time.Duration, time.Duration, error) {
    var amount time.Duration
    var unit string
    _, err := fmt.Sscanf(query, "%d %s", &amount, &unit)
    if err != nil {
        return time.Duration(0), time.Duration(0), err
    }

    // weeks -> week
    unit = strings.TrimSuffix(unit, "s")

    d, ok := unitNames[unit]
    if !ok {
        err := fmt.Errorf("unknown duration: %q", unit) // <1>
        return time.Duration(0), time.Duration(0), err
    }
    // Negative duration since times are offset from now
    return -(amount * d), d, nil
}
```

You also need roundTime, which will round time to a specific time delta:

types/time/parse_time/parse_time.go
```go
// roundTime rounds time to delta frequency.
func roundTime(t time.Time, delta time.Duration) time.Time {
    year, month, day := t.Year(), t.Month(), t.Day()
    hour, minute := t.Hour(), t.Minute()

    switch {
    case delta >= time.Hour:
        minute = 0
        fallthrough
    case delta >= 24*time.Hour:
        minute, hour = 0, 0
    }

    return time.Date(year, month, day, hour, minute, 0, 0, t.Location())
}
```

Finally, you can write parseTime:

types/time/parse_time/parse_time.go
```go
// parseTime parses a time query (such as "2 weeks ago", "today GMT" ...)
// and will return the corresponding time
func parseTime(query string) (time.Time, error) {
    loc, query, err := extractLocation(query)
    if err != nil {
        return time.Time{}, err
    }

    if query == "today" {
        return today(loc), nil
    }

    // Try YYYY-mm-ddTHH:MM first
    t, err := time.ParseInLocation("2006-01-02T15:04", query, loc)
    if err == nil {
        return t, nil
    }

    delta, round, err := parseDelta(query)
    if err != nil {
        return time.Time{}, err
    }

    t = time.Now().In(loc).Add(delta) // .In converts time zones
    return roundTime(t, round), nil
}
```

Discussion

Go's time.Time has support for time zones (called time.Location). To load time zone information, Go will use the time zone database on your computer. Make sure to update this database on your servers.

Dockerizing Time

 If you build a docker container for your Go program, make sure the time zone information is found there. Some small base images like scratch or busybox do not come with the time zone information database by default.

Since Go 1.15, there's a time/tzdata module that can be used to embed the time zone information in your program.

You're using a regular expression to find out the time zone. See *Using Regular Expressions to Convert camelCase to lower_with_underscore* for another example on using regular expressions.

In today, you use the time.Time.In method to convert the current time to the required time zone.

You write your own parseDelta since the built-in time.PraseDuration is missing days and weeks. time.ParseDuration also uses more developer-oriented names, such as ns or μs.

Initially, you might want to use time.Time.Truncate, but when you read its documentation you see this:

> Truncate operates on the time as an absolute duration since the zero time; it does not operate on the presentation form of the time. Thus, Truncate(Hour) may return a time with a non-zero minute, depending on the time's location.

You write your own roundTime to round a time for a specific duration.

Time seems simple. When asked, "What's the time?" you look at your smart phone or watch and tell the current time. Under the hood, things are much more complicated.

Computers don't know about time; they know about frequency (CPU cycles) and about numbers. Internally, computers store time as the number of seconds elapsed since January 1, 1970 (GMT). This specific time is called epoch or unix[4] time.

---

4. https://unixtime.org/

Year 2038 Problem

Around 3 a.m. on January 19, 2038, time stored on 32-bit machines will overflow. This is going to cause a huge problem, though a lot of people are working hard to make sure nothing bad will happen because of it.

You might think 2038 is a long way off, but remember the warning, "Dates on calendars are closer than they appear." (I truly hope I will finish this book before 2038.)

If you're curious, read more about the 2038 problem at https://computer.howstuffworks.com/question75.htm. The world is divided into time zones, and converting between time zones is something developers love to hate.

Time is not always linear. We move the clock back one hour in the fall and forward one hour in the spring. And to make things worse, every country does it on a different date. An external database holds when each country is moving to daylight saving time and back—hopefully it's updated on your machine.

Another reason for time "jumping" in your computer can be an update from an NTP[5] server. Unlike daylight saving time, updates can happen daily.

You'll find more oddities about computers and time. If you're curious, head over to "Falsehoods programmers believe about time"[6] and "Falsehoods programmers believe about time zones,"[7] and have fun reading the impressive list compiled there and in the follow-up posts.

Go's time.Time and time.Duration should be enough for all your timely needs. But you need to understand the underlying complexities of time to work with it effectively.

Final Thoughts

The Go language and its standard library come with many useful types and their associated functions and methods. Most of these types are simple to use, but as usual with computers, you should be aware of some edge cases.

---

5.   https://www.ntp.org/documentation/4.2.8-series/
6.   https://infiniteundo.com/post/25326999628/falsehoods-programmers-believe-about-time
7.   https://www.zainrizvi.io/blog/falsehoods-programmers-believe-about-time-zones/

With slices, you saw that you need to understand how they and append are implemented in order to work with them effectively. And with time, you saw that you need to know the underlying complexity of time and computers to get correct results when working with it.

## CHAPTER 7

Working with Structs, Methods, and Interfaces

Go doesn't offer a traditional object-oriented programming (OO) like Java, C++, or Python does.

OO is a tool to model code. It's not the "one true way," as some people try to make it. The Go development team took a long look at many years of OO languages and found a unique approach that works well with the Go ideology.

In this chapter, we are going to explore the tools that compose Go's data-oriented programming (as Bill Kennedy calls it)—structs, methods, and interfaces. We'll also see how you can use generics to reduce code size and increase type safety.

Recipe 37

Using Ad Hoc Interfaces

Task

You're working on developer tools in your company. Brenda, the group lead, assigns the following issue to you:

> The current logger doesn't flush logs, which makes it hard to look at logs as they appear. Please make the logger flush logs, but only if the underlying writer supports it.

After getting some coffee, you start digging at the current log implementation.

You find Logger with several log levels:

oo/logger/logger.go

```go
// Level is a log level.
type Level byte

const (
    Debug Level = iota + 1
    Info
    Error
)

func (l Level) String() string {
    switch l {
    case Debug:
        return "DEBUG"
    case Info:
        return "INFO"
    case Error:
        return "ERROR"
    }

    return fmt.Sprintf("Level <%d>", l)
}

type Logger struct {
    level Level
    w     io.Writer
}

func NewLogger(level Level, out io.Writer) Logger {
    l := Logger{level, out}
    return l
}
```

Next is a utility method that does the actual logging:

oo/logger/logger.go

```go
func (l Logger) log(level Level, format string, args ...any) {
    if level < l.level {
        return
    }

    msg := fmt.Sprintf(format, args...)
    ts := time.Now().UTC().Format(time.RFC3339)
    fmt.Fprintf(l.w, "[%s] - %s - %s\n", ts, level, msg)
}
```

Finally, you see the top-level API methods:

oo/logger/logger.go
```
// Debug is a debug log.
func (l Logger) Debug(format string, args ...any) {
    l.log(Debug, format, args...)
}

// Info is an info log.
func (l Logger) Info(format string, args ...any) {
    l.log(Info, format, args...)
}

// Error is an error log.
func (l Logger) Error(format string, args ...any) {
    l.log(Error, format, args...)
}
```

Solution

You write the following ad hoc syncer interface:

oo/logger/fix/logger.go
```
type syncer interface {
    Sync() error
}
```

You also define a nopSyncer that implements the syncer interface without doing anything.

The NOP Term

The term NOP means "no operation." It originated in assembly language (see https://www.intel.com/content/www/us/en/docs/programmable/683620/current/nop.html)) but is commonly used for types/functions that do nothing.

You add an s field to the Logger:

oo/logger/fix/logger.go
```
// Logger is a logger.
type Logger struct {
    level Level
    w     io.Writer
    s syncer
}
```

In NewLogger you initially set w to a nopSyncer, then if the w parameter also implements the syncer interface, you set it to w:

oo/logger/fix/logger.go
```
// NewLogger returns a new logger with level and output.
func NewLogger(level Level, out io.Writer) Logger {
    log := Logger{level, out, nopSyncer{}}
    if s, ok := out.(syncer); ok {
        log.s = s
    }
    return log
}
```

And finally, in the log utility method, call s.Sync():

oo/logger/fix/logger.go
```
func (l Logger) log(level Level, format string, args ...any) {
    if l.level > level {
        return
    }

    msg := fmt.Sprintf(format, args...)
    ts := time.Now().UTC().Format(time.RFC3339)
    fmt.Fprintf(l.w, "[%s] - %s - %s\n", ts, level, msg)

    l.s.Sync()
}
```

Discussion

A Go Proverb
by: Rob Pike

The bigger the interface, the weaker the abstraction.

Another option you considered was to define a WriteSyncer interface that embeds the io.Writer interface and adds a Sync method, such as the one os.File has:

```
type WriteSyncer interface {
    io.Writer
    Sync() error
}
```

However, this will limit the number of types that can be used as the log destination (w).

By defining the syncer interface and checking that w implements it, you support a wider range of types that have a Sync method—not only *os.File.

By using the comma, ok version of type assertion, you avoid panics if type underlying w does not implement syncer.

Recipe 38

Wrapping the http.ResponseWriter Interface

Task

You're responsible for an internal web service that answers time-related queries, such as time zone offsets, via HTTP.

When you arrive in the morning, you see the following email:

> Hi all,
>
> We (the operations team) are starting to standardize service monitoring. HTTP servers must log an error every time the handler returns an HTTP error code (>= 400). Please try to have this ready by the end of the month.

You convert this email to an issue, assign it to yourself, and start working.

Solution

You start by writing an errWriter struct that will implement the http.ResponseWriter interface:

oo/logerr/httpd.go
```
type errWriter struct {
    http.ResponseWriter
    statusCode int
}

func (ew *errWriter) WriteHeader(statusCode int) {
    ew.statusCode = statusCode
    ew.ResponseWriter.WriteHeader(statusCode)
}
```

Then you write an HTTP handler function that will replace the original http.ResponseWriter passed to the handler with an errWriter and will then log a possible error after the original handler has returned:

oo/logerr/httpd.go
```
func logErr(w http.ResponseWriter, r *http.Request) {
    ew := errWriter{ResponseWriter: w}
    http.DefaultServeMux.ServeHTTP(&ew, r)

    if ew.statusCode >= http.StatusBadRequest {
        log.Printf("error: %s %s <%d>", r.Method, r.URL.Path, ew.statusCode)
    }
}
```

Finally, you start the built-in HTTP server with logErr as the global HTTP handler:

```
oo/logerr/httpd.go
func main() {
    http.HandleFunc(offsetPrefix, offsetHandler)

    handler := http.HandlerFunc(logErr)
    if err := http.ListenAndServe(":8080", handler); err != nil {
        log.Fatalf("error: %s", err)
    }
}
```

For completeness, here's the rest of the code:

```
oo/logerr/httpd.go
func tzOffset(name string) (int, error) {
    loc, err := time.LoadLocation(name)
    if err != nil {
        return 0, err
    }

    _, offset := time.Now().In(loc).Zone()
    return offset, nil
}

const (
    offsetPrefix = "/offset/"
)

func offsetHandler(w http.ResponseWriter, r *http.Request) {
    // "/offset/US/Pacific" -> "US/Pacific"
    name := r.URL.Path[len(offsetPrefix):]
    offset, err := tzOffset(name)
    if err != nil {
        errMsg := fmt.Sprintf("unknown offset - %q", name)
        http.Error(w, errMsg, http.StatusNotFound)
        return
    }

    fmt.Fprintf(w, "%d\n", offset)
}
```

Discussion

errWriter embeds an http.ResponseWriter, and by doing so it implements the http.ResponseWriter interface as well. You pass an errWriter as the w argument (of type http.ResponseWriter) to the ServeHTTP method of the http.DefaultServeMux. Somewhere inside the ServeHTTP method, it'll call the w.WriteHeader, and Go will resolve it to the errWriter.WriteHeader. Your errWriter.WriteHeader method stores the status code in the statusCode field and then calls the embedded http.ResponseWriter.WriteHeader.

All other w methods the mux ServeHTTP calls will be resolved to the embedded ResponseWriter.

The logErr function is used as a global http.Handler passed to http.ListenAndServe. Every HTTP request will be directed to logErr, which will replace the provided http.ResponseWriter with an errWriter and pass the request to the http.DefaultServeMux. If the response code signals an error, it'll log the error.

You don't need to implement every method in the interface you're implementing. You can embed another value implementing this interface and implement only the methods you need to change. Note that this is not the classic OO inheritance—the receiver in the other methods invoked by the interface is the embedded type, not your type.

Recipe 39

Using Generics to Reduce Code Size

Task

During coffee, you have a discussion with Mark from the data science team.

When you come back, you open a chat with Heather, your team lead:

> Just had an interesting discussion with Mark from the data science team. I think that with very little code we get some interesting insights from our data as well. Can I spend a couple of hours prototyping a small statistics library we can use?

Heather replies:

> Sure! Please don't spend more than half a day on it. Oh, and make sure your code works on ints *and* floats.

You smile and start coding.

Solution

You decide to write generic functions, and you start by defining the allowed types in an interface:

oo/stats/stats.go
```go
// Number is set of possible numbers.
type Number interface {
    ~float64 | ~int
}
```

Then you use this interface as a type constraint in the Max function:

oo/stats/stats.go
```go
Line 1    // Max returns the maximal value in values.
   -      func Max[T Number](values []T) (T, error) {
   -          if len(values) == 0 {
   -              var zero T
   5              return zero, fmt.Errorf("Max of empty slice")
   -          }
   -
   -          max := values[0]
   -          for _, v := range values[1:] {
   10             if v > max {
   -                  max = v
   -              }
   -          }
   -          return max, nil
   15     }
```

Now you can use Max both on an []int and a []float64:

oo/stats/example_test.go
```go
Line 1    func ExampleMax() {
   -          iVals := []int{15, 42, 16, 8, 23, 4}
   -          fmt.Println(Max(iVals))
   -
   5          fVals := []float64{3.14, 2.718, 6.283, 1.618}
   -          fmt.Println(Max(fVals))
   -
   -          _, err := Max[int](nil)
   -          fmt.Println(err)
   10
   -          // Output:
   -          // 42 <nil>
   -          // 6.283 <nil>
   -          // Max of empty slice
   15     }
```

Discussion

By using generics, you're able to write a single function that handles both ints and floats.

The Number interface is a constraint on types. The ~ means that not only int is allowed but also any other types that are basically an int (for example, type Level int).

In line 4, we solve the problem of returning zero value when there's an error. Since T can be either an int or a float64 (and maybe also a string in later versions), you can't use 0. Once we declare var zero T, then zero will be initialized to the zero value for T and the compiler will be happy.

In line 8, you need to explicitly tell the Go compiler which version of Max you want since nil is untyped. In the two cases before, the compiler is able to deduce the version of Max to use from the input parameter.

To learn more about generics, I recommend reading (or watching) "When to Use Generics"[1] by Ian Lance Taylor of the Go team.

You can also look at the following experimental packages in the golang.org/x repository:

- golang.org/x/exp/maps
- golang.org/x/exp/slices
- golang.org/x/exp/constraints

These packages might give you ideas on how to use generics.

Recipe 40

Using Generics for Type-Safe Data Structures

Task

You're helping the operations team to gather metrics on running servers.

Jack comes over and says:

> We need to calculate the mean of the last N samples. The samples can be various types of numbers, including time.Duration.

You discuss the API with Jack, write the design decision in the issue, and start coding.

---

1.   https://go.dev/blog/when-generics

Solution

You start by defining what a number is, using the Number interface, and then a Ring struct, which will be a circular ring buffer:

oo/ring/ring.go
```
Line 1  // Number is set of possible numbers.
-       type Number interface {
-           ~int | ~int16 | ~int32 | ~int64 |
-               ~uint | ~uint16 | ~uint32 | ~uint64 |
5               ~float32 | ~float64
-       }
-
-       // Ring is a circular ring buffer.
-       type Ring[T Number] struct {
10          size    int
-           i       int
-           values  []T
-       }
```

Next, you write the NewRing function, which creates a new Ring:

oo/ring/ring.go
```
// NewRing returns a new Ring.
func NewRing[T Number](size int) (*Ring[T], error) {
    if size <= 0 {
        return nil, fmt.Errorf("size must be > 0")
    }

    r := Ring[T]{
        size:   size,
        values: make([]T, size),
    }
    return &r, nil
}
```

Then you write the Push method, which adds a value to the ring. If there are more values than the ring size, the last value will be overwritten:

oo/ring/ring.go
```
// Push pushes item to the ring, possibly overwriting an old value.
func (r *Ring[T]) Push(v T) {
    r.values[r.i] = v
    r.i = (r.i + 1) % r.size
}
```

And lastly, you write the Mean method, which computes the mean of the current values in the ring:

oo/ring/ring.go
```
// Mean returns the mean of values in the ring.
func (r *Ring[T]) Mean() float64 {
    var s T = 0
    for _, v := range r.values {
        s += v
    }

    return float64(s) / float64(r.size)
}
```

You write a short example test to document and also test your code:

oo/ring/example_test.go
```
func ExampleRing() {
    size := 4
    r, err := NewRing[int](size)
    if err != nil {
        fmt.Printf("error: %s", err)
        return
    }

    for i := 1; i <= 10; i++ {
        r.Push(i)
    }
    fmt.Println(r.Mean())

    // Output:
    // 8.5
}
```

Discussion

Before Go 1.18 and generics, your only option to write a generic collection was to use any for the values. Using any bypasses the type system—you can push a string to a ring of integers. Furthermore, when you calculate Mean, you need to do a type assertion from any to a number type; otherwise, you won't be able to add values.

In line 9 we declare the struct as having generics type T, and in line 12 we use T for the values.

Generic structures have limits—you cannot write generic methods with types other than T. In practice, I don't find this limitation that problematic.

Recipe 41

Using Generics for Better Type Safety

Task

You just became the owner of a legacy server that grew to be complex and contains a lot of code. You dig through the issues for patterns and open the following issue:

> There are several bugs (1934, 2013, 2083, 2111) that are related. In all of them, the underlying issue was that someone sent a non-pointer to json.Unmarshal. I plan to add a utility function called UnmarshalJSON that will validate that the value sent to json.Unmarshal is a pointer.

You show this to your boss, Peter, and he says, "Go for it."

Solution

First you define what types are valid for JSON decoding.

oo/decode/decode.go
```
// UserRequest is a request for user information.
type UserRequest struct {
    Login string
}

// GroupRequest is a request for group information.
type GroupRequest struct {
    ID string
}

// Request is the set of all possible requests.
type Request interface {
    UserRequest | GroupRequest
}
```

And then you write UnmarshalJSON, which accepts pointers from valid types:

oo/decode/decode.go
```
Line 1  // UnmarshalJSON implements json.Unmarshaler.
     2  func UnmarshalJSON[T Request](data []byte, d *T) error {
     3      return json.Unmarshal(data, d)
     4  }
```

Discussion

The encoding/json package, as well as other serialization packages, was written before Go got generics. To be able to support various types, the functions in encoding/json accept any (previously interface{}). Accepting any means the Go compiler cannot type check the arguments passed to these functions. The function does type-checking at runtime, using reflection. We gained flexibility but lost type safety.

Now that we have generics, we can get the flexibility *and* the type safety.

The *T in line 2 means that the type must be a pointer.

This means that this code will compile:

```
data := []byte(`{"login": "elliot"}`)
var r UserRequest
DecodeJSON(data, &r)
```

But the following code will fail to compile:

```
data := []byte(`{"login": "elliot"}`)
var r UserRequest
DecodeJSON(data, r) // Won't compile, not a pointer.
```

Final Thoughts

Go has an untraditional object-oriented system that will force you to change the way you think about modeling software.

Go's OO system is simple but powerful. Learn how to use it effectively, and after a while you'll stop missing features from other traditional OO languages.

Remember the rule of thumb: *accept interface, return types*. For example, os.Open returns *os.File, and io.Copy accepts io.Writer and io.Reader. Following this rule is the first step toward writing idiomatic Go code.

Next, we'll look at how Go handles errors—don't panic!

## CHAPTER 8

Working with Errors

In Go, we treat errors as values, not as exceptions to be raised or thrown. In this chapter, we'll look at some best practices for working with errors. Knowing how to effectively work with errors will do wonders for both the readability of your code and its resilience to errors.

Recipe 42

Handling and Returning Errors

Task

You're working in the ops team. Beth, the ops lead, assigns the following issue to you:

> All of your services run as daemons and write their process ID (PID) to a file. Write a utility function that will read the PID from a file, issue a kill command to terminate the server, and then remove the PID file.

You go to the kitchen and discuss how to implement this with Sam, your co-worker, over green tea. As you leave, he says, "Don't forget about error handling."

Solution

You start by defining a killServer function that gets a file name and returns an error:

```
errors/kill_server/kill_server.go
func killServer(pidFile string) error {
```

The first step is to open the file:

errors/kill_server/kill_server.go
```
file, err := os.Open(pidFile)
if err != nil {
    return fmt.Errorf("can't open PID file: %w", err)
}
defer file.Close()
```

Then you read the process ID from the file:

errors/kill_server/kill_server.go
```
var pid int
_, err = fmt.Fscanf(file, "%d", &pid)
if err != nil {
    return fmt.Errorf("bad PID in %q: %w", pidFile, err)
}
```

Next, you remove the file:

errors/kill_server/kill_server.go
```
if err := os.Remove(pidFile); err != nil {
    log.Printf("can't remove %q - %s", pidFile, err) // warn, no error
}
```

And finally, you kill the server:

errors/kill_server/kill_server.go
```
return kill(pid)
```

Where kill is a small utility function, you write:

errors/kill_server/kill_server.go
```
func kill(pid int) error {
    proc, err := os.FindProcess(pid)
    if err != nil {
        return err
    }

    return proc.Kill()
}
```

Discussion

You use the %w verb in fmt.Errorf, which will wrap the original error with a custom error. This allows users of the function to have the full error stack and inspect it using functions from the errors package, such as errors.Is and errors.As.

When you fail to remove the PID file, you decide not to return an error but to log a warning. This is a design decision, and you should discuss this before moving on.

You *can* ignore errors, either by ignoring return values or using the _ identifier, but I highly discourage you from doing so.

Recipe 43

Handling Panics

Task

You're working on an internal search engine for your company. This morning, an email from the operations team is waiting for you:

> Hi there,
>
> Last night the search engine server crashed a couple of times. The logs point to a dist.Edit function.
>
> Please investigate, and let us know when to roll out a new version.
>
> Happy hunting,
>
> Jesse

You go over the code and find that dist.Edit is a function from an external package that computes the edit distance[1] between two strings.

You take a look at the package code, but it's tricky and unfamiliar, so you decide not to patch it. Instead, you decide to wrap the function so it won't panic but instead will return an error and handle errors in your code in an idiomatic Go way.

Solution

You start with a new function called EditDistance that returns both the distance and an error:

```
errors/leven/leven.go
// EditDistance Returns the edit (Levenshtein) distance  between s1 and s2.
// It wraps dist.Edit against panics.
func EditDistance(s1, s2 string) (distance int, err error) {
```

The function declares "named return values"—distance and err.

---

1. https://en.wikipedia.org/wiki/Levenshtein_distance

Then you use the built-in recover function inside a defer to catch a possible panic:

```
errors/leven/leven.go
defer func() {
    if e := recover(); e != nil {
        err = fmt.Errorf("%v", e) // Convert e (any) to error
    }
}()
```

Finally, you use the original dist.Edit:

```
errors/leven/leven.go
return dist.Edit(s1, s2), nil
```

Discussion

Named return values, and arguments, are just like any other function-level variable. You need to use named return values when handling panics since you don't have another way to change the output of EditDistance from inside the defer.

In case of success, err will remain with the zero value of errors, which is nil. In case of an error, e will be non-nil and you assign it to err by converting from any to error using fmt.Errorf.

The common idiom in Go is to return an error value. But in some cases, a function will panic. Sometimes people coming to Go from other languages will use panic as they would use exceptions in those languages. And sometimes, panics will happen due to plain old bugs.

In your code, you'll need to decide if you want to guard against panics or let your program crash. Use defer with recover to guard against panics.

Failing Fast

One school of programming is called "fail fast." Fail-fast systems are usually designed to stop normal operation rather than attempt to continue a possibly flawed process.

From my experience, failing fast combined with a monitoring and recovery system yields very robust systems. I highly recommend watching Joe Armstrong's talk on the subject, "Systems that Run Forever Self-Heal and Scale."[2]

---

2.   https://www.infoq.com/presentations/self-heal-scalable-system/

You can use named return values outside the scope of handling panics. I find this kind of programming hard to follow and seldom use named return values.

Handling Panics in Goroutines

Task

You are the owner of an internal library that executes jobs from a channel in goroutines. When you arrive in the morning, you see the following issue assigned to you from the operations team lead, Mia:

> Last night the system crashed several times. We triaged the bug to a new handler that panicked. We disabled the handler, and now the system runs. Please catch panics in the handlers. I don't like the sound the pager makes at 3 a.m.

Solution

You look at the code, and the main loop seems simple:

errors/drain/drain.go
```
type Message struct {
    Time time.Time
    Type string
    Data []byte
}

func drain(ch <-chan Message, handler func(Message)) {
    for msg := range ch {
        msg.Time = time.Now()
        go handler(msg)
    }
}
```

You create a test handler that will panic:

errors/drain/drain.go
```
func testHandler(msg Message) {
    ts := msg.Time.Format("15:04:03")
    log.Printf("%s: %s: %x...\n", ts, msg.Type, msg.Data[:20])
}
```

Then you run the code:

errors/drain/drain.go
```go
func main() {
    ch := make(chan Message)

    // Populate some data
    go func() {
        defer close(ch)
        for i := 0; i < 5; i++ {
            msg := Message{
                Type: "test",
                Data: []byte(fmt.Sprintf("payload %d", i)),
            }
            ch <- msg
        }
    }()

    drain(ch, testHandler)
    time.Sleep(time.Second) // let goroutines run
    fmt.Println("DONE")
}
```

And you see the problem:

```
panic: runtime error: slice bounds out of range [:20] with capacity 16

goroutine 19 [running]:
main.testHandler(0xbfd5745aa34b8eee, 0x12c99, 0x569420, 0x4cb528, \
            0x4, 0xc0000b8040, 0x9, 0x10)
        ./code/errors/drain.go:30 +0x17e
created by main.drain
        ./code/errors/drain.go:36 +0x117
```

Solution

You write safelyGo, which will launch a goroutine that wraps the handler in defer + recover:

errors/drain/fix/drain.go
```go
// safelyGo will run fn in a goroutine, and guard it from panics
func safelyGo(fn func()) {
    go func() {
        defer func() {
            if err := recover(); err != nil {
                log.Printf("error: %s", err)
            }
        }()
        fn()
    }()
}
```

And then you use it in the drain function:

```
errors/drain/fix/drain.go
func drain(ch <-chan Message, handler func(Message)) {
    for msg := range ch {
        msg.Time = time.Now()
➤       safelyGo(func() {
➤           handler(msg)
➤       })
    }
}
```

When you run the code now, you see error messages, but it runs to completion:

```
2020/10/01 07:36:06 error: runtime error: slice bounds out of range [:20] \
    with capacity 16
2020/10/01 07:36:06 error: runtime error: slice bounds out of range [:20] \
    with capacity 16
2020/10/01 07:36:06 error: runtime error: slice bounds out of range [:20] \
    with capacity 16
2020/10/01 07:36:06 error: runtime error: slice bounds out of range [:20] \
    with capacity 16
2020/10/01 07:36:06 error: runtime error: slice bounds out of range [:20] \
    with capacity 16
DONE
```

Discussion

Crashing the whole program when a goroutine panics might seems like an odd design choice, but a good reason is behind it.

When you run a thread in another programming language and it crashes, the program will continue to run. However, the program runs in a bad state, and the main program won't know that the thread is no longer running. Eventually, the program will crash, and it'll be much harder to figure the cause of the issue. See the previous Discussion, on page 122, for more information.

The Go developers believe (as do I) that it's better to crash than continue running in a bad state. It's much harder to fix bugs in the latter approach.

In some cases, you'll want to guard from panics in goroutines. A method like safelyGo can solve most of the problem. However, if the handler code is started in a different goroutine, the program will still crash. There's no bulletproof way to guard against panics.

Here's an example with the standard library HTTP server:

```
errors/drain/httpd/crasher.go
package main

import (
    "fmt"
    "log"
    "net/http"
)

func crashHandler(w http.ResponseWriter, r *http.Request) {
    go func() {
        panic("down we go!")
    }()
    fmt.Fprintln(w, "OK")
}

func main() {
    http.HandleFunc("/carsh", crashHandler)

    addr := ":8080"
    log.Printf("server starting on %s", addr)
    if err := http.ListenAndServe(addr, nil); err != nil {
        log.Fatalf("error: %s", err)
    }
}
```

If you run this code and then hit http://localhost:8080/carsh, you'll see "OK". When you try again, you'll see that the server is no longer running.

What you need is another layer that will restart crashing services. Systems such as Docker, Kubernetes, and others know how to do that. Don't forget to monitor such crashes and alter on them. See more on this at *Shipping Your Code*.

Recipe 45

Checking Errors

Task

The killServer function you wrote in *Handling and Returning Errors* is working well. You get another issue assigned to you regarding it:

> Our application is composed of several services, each storing its process ID (PID) in a file. We'd like a function to get a list of files and terminate the processes with PIDs in their files. The function should return an error for a bad PID or if it can't kill. But if the PID file is missing, ignore it.

You go out for a walk, thinking about the solution. When you come back, you start writing the code.

Solution

You decide to keep the original killServer function as is and add another, called killFromFiles:

errors/kill_server/kill_server.go
```
func killFromFiles(logFiles []string) error {
```

You run a for loop over the files:

errors/kill_server/kill_server.go
```
for _, logFile := range logFiles {
```

Then you call killServer on every file:

errors/kill_server/kill_server.go
```
err := killServer(logFile)
if err == nil {
    return nil
}
```

If there's no error, it means we managed to stop the daemon process, and we can return without an error.

If there is an error, you check if it's an os.PathError:

errors/kill_server/kill_server.go
```
if !errors.Is(err, os.ErrNotExist) { // File not found
    return err
}
```

The errors.As function will succeed if the error or one of the errors it wraps is an os.PathError.

Finally, when the for loop is exhausted, it means we couldn't find any file. You construct a new error:

errors/kill_server/kill_server.go
```
files := strings.Join(logFiles, ", ")
return fmt.Errorf("no existing file found: %v", files)
```

Discussion

By using functions from the errors package, you can inspect errors and the errors they wrap, find a specific error, and have better error handling in your code.

I encourage you to read the errors package documentation and play with the example to see how you can utilize these functions.

Wrapping Errors

Task

As the new head of the Go guild in the company, you interview your fellow developers. A common theme that comes up is that they are missing context information from errors. For example, Helen said this:

> In Python, when there's an exception I can see the whole call stack, including file names and line numbers. In Go, I only see the error text and maybe the chain of errors. This makes it hard to debug, mostly in low-level functions that are called from many places.

You reach out to your boss and ask her if it's OK to add some call stack information to some errors. She says, "OK, but make sure it's not slowing us down too much."

Solution

After reading the runtime package documentation, you start to code.

First you define a Wrapper struct that will add call information to an existing error.

```
errors/wrap/wrap.go
// Wrapper wraps an error with call stack information.
type Wrapper struct {
    error
    stack []uintptr
}

// Unwrap returns the wrapped error.
func (w *Wrapper) Unwrap() error {
    return w.error
}
```

Then you define a Frame struct, which is the call location:

errors/wrap/wrap.go
```
// Frame is a call location.
type Frame struct {
    Function string
    File     string
    Line     int
}

var pathSep = string(os.PathSeparator)

func trimPath(path string, size int) string {
    fields := strings.Split(path, pathSep)
    if n := len(fields); n > size {
        fields = fields[len(fields)-size:]
    }
    return strings.Join(fields, pathSep)
}

func (f Frame) String() string {
    return fmt.Sprintf("%s:%d: %s", trimPath(f.File, 3), f.Line, f.Function)
}
```

Next you write a Wrap function that will wrap an error and add caller information:

errors/wrap/wrap.go
```
Line 1  // Wrap wraps an error with call stack information.
    -   func Wrap(err error) error {
            const depth = 32
            var pcs [depth]uintptr
    5       n := runtime.Callers(2, pcs[:])

            w := Wrapper{
                error: err,
                stack: pcs[:n],
    10      }
            return &w
    -   }
```

Finally, you add a Stack method to Wrapper that will return a slice of frames:

errors/wrap/wrap.go
```
// Stack returns the call stack, innermost frame first.
func (w *Wrapper) Stack() []Frame {
    locs := make([]Frame, 0, len(w.stack))
    frames := runtime.CallersFrames(w.stack)
    for {
        frame, more := frames.Next()
        loc := Frame{
            Function: frame.Function,
            File:     frame.File,
            Line:     frame.Line,
        }
```

```
        locs = append(locs, loc)
        if !more {
            break
        }
    }
    return locs
}
```

Discussion

One of Go's proverbs is "errors are values." This means that errors are cheap, and you pass them around just like any other value. Exceptions in other programming languages tend to be more expensive to create.

In the Wrap function, you get only the program counters (PC) for the current call. You defer the work of getting function name, file name, and line number to when the user calls the Stack method.

The Wrapper struct embeds an error. This means it implements the error interface, and calling the embedded Error method will return the original error message.

The 2 in line 5 means how many inner functions to skip. If you pass 0, you'll get runtime.Callers and Wrap in the result, which will probably confuse the users.

Users of your code can choose which errors to wrap and will probably avoid doing so in performance-sensitive places.

Once a user sees a stack trace, they'll think your program crashed. Save the stack traces to a log file, and print out only the error message to the user.

---

pkg/errors

Dave Cheney, one of Go community's more pragmatic members, wrote pkg/errors. This package influenced the current design of the errors package in Go version 1.13.

Dave decided to archive pkg/errors. You can still use it, but there won't be any changes or bug fixes.

Final Thoughts

To newcomers, Go code is littered with error checking. It can be verbose, but from my personal experience, Go forces you to *think* about error handling more than other languages, resulting in a more robust code.

Here are some questions I ask myself when handling errors:

- Should I handle this error or pass it up to the caller?

- How can I format a clear error message?

- Should I wrap the original error? (The answer here is usually yes.)

- Are there any resources I need to close before returning an error? (defer is the usual solution.)

- Should I handle panics here?

Next, we'll look at another distinct Go feature—its concurrency support.

## CHAPTER 9

Using Goroutines, Channels, and Context for Concurrency

Go has built-in support for utilizing all the CPU cores your machine has. Writing concurrent code is hard; Go doesn't make it easy, but it makes it easier than the ways you'll find in other languages such as Java, C, Python, and others.

One of the proverbs we say in the Go community is "Don't communicate by sharing memory; share memory by communicating." This approach of sending messages between concurrency units, as opposed to shared memory and locks, is easier to work with. Sending messages between concurrency units isn't a new idea—Tony Hoare published an article about communicating sequential processes (or CSP) in 1978. Go is also not the only language to use CSP. Other languages (notably Erlang) use this method as well.

Go's concurrency units are goroutines and channels. Goroutines are light-weight independent paths of execution, and channels are typed directional pipes that you can send messages over. The community recommendation is to use channels whenever you can to communicate between goroutines. Channels seem simple, but you need to pay attention to their blocking semantics, otherwise you might get into deadlocks.

It's worth keeping in mind that concurrency is a form of optimization, and if your sequential code runs fast enough, let it be. Reasoning about and debugging concurrent code is *hard*.

Recipe 47

Converting Sequential Code to Parallel

Task

You're working on an internal application. Your current focus is on performance and stability.

Lucy, the performance team lead, sends you a link to the following issue:

> The application currently holds a list of servers it can query. When it needs to, it picks one at random and then calls its API. We started ranking the servers by access speed, but this code is sequential and takes its time. Please convert the code to concurrent.

After some thinking, you decide to start with a simple approach and use a goroutine per server.

Solution

You start by examining the current code. It defines an Info struct:

concurrency/sites_delay/sites_delay.go
```
// Info is information on site.
type Info struct {
    statusCode int
    delay      time.Duration
}
```

For a single URL, a siteInfo function returns the information about the URL:

concurrency/sites_delay/sites_delay.go
```
func siteInfo(url string) (Info, error) {
    var info Info

    start := time.Now()
    resp, err := http.Get(url)
    if err != nil {
        return info, err
    }
    defer resp.Body.Close()

    // Consume data from server
    _, err = io.Copy(io.Discard, resp.Body)
    if err != nil {
        return info, err
    }
```

```
        info.delay = time.Since(start)
        info.statusCode = resp.StatusCode
        return info, nil
}
```

And the sitesInfo function gets a slice of the URL and returns a map from the URL to its Info struct:

concurrency/sites_delay/sites_delay.go
```
func sitesInfo(urls []string) (map[string]Info, error) {
    out := make(map[string]Info)
    for _, url := range urls {
        info, err := siteInfo(url)
        if err != nil {
            return nil, err
        }
        out[url] = info
    }
    return out, nil
}
```

You start by writing some code to see the current performance:

concurrency/sites_delay/sites_delay.go
```
func main() {
    start := time.Now()

    urls := []string{
        "https://www.apple.com/",
        "https://www.microsoft.com/",
        "https://www.ibm.com/",
        "https://www.dell.com/",
    }

    infos, err := sitesInfo(urls)
    if err != nil {
        log.Fatalf("error: %s", err)
    }

    for url, info := range infos {
        fmt.Printf("%s: %+v\n", url, info)
    }

    duration := time.Since(start)
    fmt.Printf("%d sites in %v\n", len(urls), duration)
}
```

When you run the code, you see the following:

```
https://www.apple.com/: {statusCode:200 delay:396436548}
https://www.microsoft.com/: {statusCode:200 delay:1387193724}
https://www.ibm.com/: {statusCode:200 delay:617966386}
```

```
https://www.dell.com/: {statusCode:403 delay:704964939}
4 sites in 3.106657406s
```

Now that you have a baseline, you're ready to make some changes.

You start by modifying the Info struct to contain the URL and a likely error value:

concurrency/sites_delay/fix/sites_delay.go
```
// Info is information on site.
type Info struct {
    url        string
    statusCode int
    delay      time.Duration
    err        error
}
```

The siteInfo function, which works on a single URL, does not change. In sitesInfo you split the code into two parts. One starts a goroutine per URL:

concurrency/sites_delay/fix/sites_delay.go
```
ch := make(chan Info)
for _, url := range urls {
    go func(u string) {
        info, err := siteInfo(u)
        info.err = err
        info.url = u
        ch <- info
    }(url)
}
```

And a second collects the return values from the output channel:

concurrency/sites_delay/fix/sites_delay.go
```
out := make(map[string]Info)
for range urls {
    info := <-ch
    if info.err != nil {
        return nil, info.err
    }
    out[info.url] = info
}
```

Then you run the code again:

```
{url:https://www.ibm.com/ statusCode:200 delay:810431817 err:<nil>}
{url:https://www.microsoft.com/ statusCode:200 delay:1182230703 err:<nil>}
{url:https://www.apple.com/ statusCode:200 delay:335793303 err:<nil>}
{url:https://www.dell.com/ statusCode:403 delay:734982452 err:<nil>}
4 sites in 1.182363981s
```

This run took about half the time.

Discussion

Before going down the path of writing concurrent code, make sure it's going to solve a problem you have. Concurrent code is harder to understand, harder to test, and much harder to debug. If your sequential code is meeting your performance requirements, stick with it.

We don't change siteInfo at all; it's still a simple function that's easy to test.

We split sitesInfo into two parts. One starts the worker goroutines, which wrap siteInfo, populate the extra information in the Info struct, and return it over the output channel.

The second part collects the output from the goroutines from the channel. In this case, we know how many goroutines there are, so we can use for range to collect exact len(urls) results from the output channel.

We have to add fields to Info since we don't know which goroutine will terminate first—we can't match the URL to the information without this extra information.

Go makes it easy to utilize all of your cores and run code concurrently.

Amdahl's Law

 Amdahl's law is a formula that gives the theoretical speedup you can gain from converting your code from sequential to parallel. I highly recommend you read about it. You'll understand that parallelism isn't "magic" and won't solve all of your performance issues. Head over to https://en.wikipedia.org/wiki/Amdahl%27s_law and start reading!

Recipe 48

Limiting the Number of Goroutines with a Buffered Channel

Task

You're working on the web server group.

Some of the pages display images, and the front-end team would like to have a uniform size for all the images. The images are imported in a batch from a local directory, and your task is to resize all images in a given directory to a given size.

Zuri, the team architect, adds the following note to the issue:

> We would like to have these resize batches run as fast as possible, so please use concurrency. However, keep in mind that resizing images is a CPU-intensive operation—there's no use running more goroutines than the number of cores.

After some searching, you find out golang.org/x/image/draw can handle resizing. For the first iteration, the team agrees you can handle only PNG files.

Solution

You start by writing a scaleFile function that will resize a single file:

concurrency/scale/scale.go
```go
func scaleFile(srcPath, destPath string, size image.Rectangle) error {
    file, err := os.Open(srcPath)
    if err != nil {
        return err
    }
    defer file.Close()

    src, err := png.Decode(file)
    if err != nil {
        return fmt.Errorf("%q - can't decode as PNG - %w", srcPath, err)
    }

    dest := image.NewRGBA(size)
    bounds := src.Bounds()
    draw.NearestNeighbor.Scale(dest, size, src, bounds, draw.Over, nil)

    out, err := os.Create(destPath)
    if err != nil {
        return err
    }
    defer out.Close()

    if err := png.Encode(out, dest); err != nil {
        out.Close()
        os.Remove(destPath)
        return err
    }

    return nil
}
```

Now you can start writing scaleDir, which will use goroutines:

concurrency/scale/scale.go
```go
func scaleDir(srcDir, destDir string, size image.Rectangle) error {
    var mu sync.Mutex
    var errs error
```

```go
    pool := make(chan bool, runtime.GOMAXPROCS(0))
    var wg sync.WaitGroup

    srcFiles, err := filepath.Glob(filepath.Join(srcDir, "*.png"))
    if err != nil {
        return err
    }

    wg.Add(len(srcFiles))
    for _, src := range srcFiles {
        go func(srcFile string) {
            defer wg.Done()

            pool <- true
            defer func() { <-pool }()

            destFile := path.Join(destDir, filepath.Base(srcFile))
            if err := scaleFile(srcFile, destFile, size); err != nil {
                mu.Lock()
                errs = errors.Join(errs, err)
                mu.Unlock()
            }
        }(src)
    }
    wg.Wait()
    return errs
}
```

Discussion

As Zuri said, in CPU-bound code, there's no use running more goroutines than the number of cores. You can find out the number of cores you have by calling runtime.GOMAXPROCS(0). Calling runtime.GOMAXPROCS with a number that is bigger than 0 will limit the parallelism of your application.

You use a buffered channel to limit the number of cores. The worker goroutine first sends to the channel; it will get blocked on sending if the channel buffer is full. You make sure that the goroutine will free a slot in the buffer by using a defer statement. Once the worker goroutine receives from the channel, another goroutine that is blocked on sending will be freed.

You also use a sync.WaitGroup to wait for all the goroutines and errors.Join to combine all the errors from the goroutines.

Using a Worker Pool with Channels

Task

As part of the site reliability engineering (SRE) team, you're working on a system to monitor your services. Ali, the SRE team lead, assigns you the following issue:

> We'd like to monitor web servers. You should report the HTTP status code and how much time it took to read the data sent from the server. Since there are many sites to monitor, please limit the amount of concurrency units you are using.

After a discussion with the team, you decide to give the user the option to specify how many units of concurrency (goroutines) they want.

Looking at the code, you find there's already a siteInfo function:

concurrency/site_worker/site_worker.go
```go
// Info is information on site.
type Info struct {
    statusCode int
    delay      time.Duration
}

func siteInfo(url string) (Info, error) {
    var info Info

    start := time.Now()
    resp, err := http.Get(url)
    if err != nil {
        return info, err
    }
    defer resp.Body.Close()

    // Consume data from server
    _, err = io.Copy(io.Discard, resp.Body)
    if err != nil {
        return info, err
    }

    info.delay = time.Since(start)
    info.statusCode = resp.StatusCode
    return info, nil
}
```

Since this function is already in use, you decide to keep it and write concurrency around it.

Start Sequential

 Start with sequential code and keep it around. It's much easier to reason about, test, and debug sequential code. If you're lucky, the sequential code will be fast enough, and you won't have to write concurrent code.

Solution

You decide to have a pool of goroutines. These goroutines will receive jobs to perform from a work queue channel and will send the results into a different—output—channel.

You start by adding wrapping Info with a workerInfo that has an err field:

concurrency/site_worker/site_worker.go
```
type workerInfo struct {
    Info
    err error
}
```

Then you write the infoReq struct that will hold the parameters a worker needs:

concurrency/site_worker/site_worker.go
```
type infoReq struct {
    url string          // URL to query
    ch  chan<- workerInfo // return channel
}
```

Now you can write the worker goroutine code:

concurrency/site_worker/site_worker.go
```
func infoWorker(ch <-chan infoReq) {
    for req := range ch {
        log.Printf("info request for: %s", req.url)
        info, err := siteInfo(req.url)
        log.Printf("%s: %#v (err=%v)", req.url, info, err)
        winfo := workerInfo{
            Info: info,
            err:  err,
        }
        req.ch <- winfo
    }
}
```

Next, you define a Pool that holds a pool of workers. In NewPool you start the worker goroutines:

concurrency/site_worker/site_worker.go

```go
// Pool is a fixed pool of workers.
type Pool struct {
    queue chan infoReq
}

// NewPool creates a new Pool with n workers.
func NewPool(n int) (*Pool, error) {
    if n <= 0 {
        return nil, fmt.Errorf("n must be > 0 (got %d)", n)
    }

    queue := make(chan infoReq)
    for i := 0; i < n; i++ {
        go infoWorker(queue)
    }

    p := Pool{
        queue: queue,
    }

    return &p, nil
}

// Close signals the worker goroutines to terminate.
func (p *Pool) Close() error {
    if p.queue != nil {
        close(p.queue)
        p.queue = nil
    }
    return nil
}
```

Finally, you can write SiteInfo, which will send a request over the work queue and will wait for the result by receiving from the return channel:

concurrency/site_worker/site_worker.go

```go
// SiteInfo returns a channel with info.
func (p *Pool) SiteInfo(url string) (Info, error) {
    // Return channel, buffered to avoid goroutine leak
    ch := make(chan workerInfo, 1)
    p.queue <- infoReq{url, ch}
    info := <-ch
    return info.Info, info.err
}
```

Discussion

Goroutines are cheap, and in most cases you can start as many as you want. But in some cases, when they are using resources such as HTTP requests, you need to limit the number of these goroutines.

One of the common methods to limit the number of goroutines is to use a worker pool. Pool.SiteInfo looks like a regular method—it gets a parameter and returns a value (and an error value), but behind the scenes it uses a pool of goroutines.

When working with a worker pool, you need to send all the information the worker needs to the worker, and you need *some* way of getting back the results. A channel is a great fit for this task. You use one channel, queue, as the incoming channel and all workers are listening on it.

The return channel in line 4 is *buffered*, which means the worker goroutine won't block sending on the channel.

Buffered channels are used to avoid blocking and also to prevent goroutine leaks. A goroutine leak is what happens when a goroutine is blocked on a channel forever. When a goroutine is blocked on a channel, the channel can't be claimed by the garbage collector since there's a reference to it from the goroutine. And the goroutine also consumes some memory for the stack. As Dave Cheney says, "Never start a goroutine without knowing how it will stop."

When a function parameter or a struct field is a channel, you can specify the direction (sending or receiving) the channel should use. Try to add this direction annotation to your channels; it will help the compiler detect errors in your program, for example, when trying to send on a receive channel.

Recipe 50

Using context.Context for Timeouts

Task

Your team is happy with your implementation of SiteInfo, and production is showing a healthier network. You're now tasked with another feature request—add a timeout to SiteInfo. If the request takes more than a specific amount of time, you should return an error.

Solution

You start by adding a context.Context field to infoReq:

concurrency/site_worker/timeout/site_worker.go

```
type infoReq struct {
    ctx context.Context
    url string            // URL to query
    ch  chan<- workerInfo // return channel
}
```

Then you start looking at all the places where there might be a timeout. You start with infoWorker:

concurrency/site_worker/timeout/site_worker.go

```
Line 1  func infoWorker(ch <-chan infoReq) {
   -        for req := range ch {
   -            log.Printf("info request for: %s", req.url)
   -            outCh := make(chan workerInfo, 1)
   5            go func() {
   -
   -                info, err := siteInfo(req.ctx, req.url)
   -                log.Printf("%s: %#v (err=%v)", req.url, info, err)
   -                winfo := workerInfo{
   10                   Info: info,
   -                    err:  err,
   -                }
   -                outCh <- winfo
   -            }()
   15
   -            select {
   -            case info := <-outCh:
   -                log.Printf("%s: %#v", req.url, info)
   -                req.ch <- info
   20           case <-req.ctx.Done():
   -                req.ch <- workerInfo{err: req.ctx.Err()}
   -            }
   -        }
   -  }
```

And then you move to SiteInfo, both when enqueuing the request and when receiving the result:

concurrency/site_worker/timeout/site_worker.go

```
Line 1  // SiteInfo return a channel with info.
   -  func (p *Pool) SiteInfo(ctx context.Context, url string) (Info, error) {
   -      // Return channel, buffered to avoid goroutine leak
   -      ch := make(chan workerInfo, 1)
   5
   -      // Send timeout
```

```
        select {
        case p.queue <- infoReq{ctx, url, ch}:
            // Nothing to do here
10      case <-ctx.Done():
            return Info{}, ctx.Err()
        }

        // Receive timeout
15      select {
        case info := <-ch:
            return info.Info, nil
        case <-ctx.Done():
            return Info{}, ctx.Err()
20      }
    }
```

Finally, you make the lower-level siteInfo use the context as well:

concurrency/site_worker/timeout/site_worker.go

```go
// Info is information on site.
type Info struct {
    statusCode int
    delay      time.Duration
}

func siteInfo(ctx context.Context, url string) (Info, error) {
    var info Info

    req, err := http.NewRequestWithContext(ctx, http.MethodGet, url, nil)
    if err != nil {
        return Info{}, nil
    }

    start := time.Now()
    resp, err := http.DefaultClient.Do(req)
    if err != nil {
        return info, err
    }
    defer resp.Body.Close()

    // Consume data from server
    _, err = io.Copy(io.Discard, resp.Body)
    if err != nil {
        return info, err
    }

    info.delay = time.Since(start)
    info.statusCode = resp.StatusCode
    return info, nil
}
```

Discussion

The context.Context interface contains a Done method that returns a channel. You can use the built-in select statement to implement a timeout, and select will block until one of the case statements is available.

In SiteInfo you use select twice: first in line 7 to check for a timeout when enqueuing the request for the worker and then in line 15 to check for a worker timeout.

The Go documentation on the context package says:

> Do not store contexts inside a struct type; instead, pass a context explicitly to each function that needs it. The context should be the first parameter, typically named ctx.

We follow this advice with SiteInfo. To send the context to the worker, we add it as a field in infoReq, which serves as parameters.

The decision to accept a context.Context in SiteInfo and not a timeout gives users more options for canceling the operation.

They can provide a context with a deadline or a timeout, or just use the context's cancel function to stop the operation.

Note that even if the context is done, the goroutine in line 5 will continue to work and issue an HTTP call. There's no way to cancel a goroutine from the outside.

Once you start with a top-level context, you need to pass it down throughout all the utility functions. Passing the context around might be tedious, but it will make you code-aware about timeouts.

The net/http package was written before context was added to the standard library. Due to the Go 1 compatibility promise, the net/http API did not change. Use http.NewRequestWithContext to create a request with a timeout, and then use the http.Client.Do method.

I can guarantee that at one point or another, your networking code *will* encounter a timeout.

Recipe 51

Passing Logger with Request ID in Context

Task

You're working on an API web server that handles various clients. Talking to your teammate Aaron over lunch, you decide to add a request ID to all the logs so it'll be easier to track a specific request. Currently the logs are all mixed up since HTTP handlers run in parallel.

After a discussion with your team lead, you open an issue, assign it to yourself, and start thinking.

Solution

To generate a unique identifier per request, you decide to use a library that doesn't require a central lock or a database. After checking several packages, you decide to use the github.com/rs/xid external package.

You write a newID() function:

```
concurrency/ctx_log/ctx_log.go
func newID() string {
    return xid.New().String()
}
```

Since you already use context.Context for timeouts and cancellation, you decide to use it to pass a logger as well. You define a Values struct and key type for storing the logger in the context:

```
concurrency/ctx_log/ctx_log.go
type ctxKey string

const (
    valuesKey ctxKey = "ctxArgs"
)

type Values struct {
    RequestID string
    Logger    *log.Logger
}
```

Then you create a function that will create a new logger with an identifier prefix:

concurrency/ctx_log/ctx_log.go
```
func idLogger(id string) *log.Logger {
    prefix := fmt.Sprintf("<%s> %s", id, log.Prefix())
    return log.New(log.Writer(), prefix, log.Flags())
}
```

You also write a function that will extract the logger from the context:

concurrency/ctx_log/ctx_log.go
```
Line 1  func ctxLogger(ctx context.Context) *log.Logger {
    -       vals, ok := ctx.Value(valuesKey).(*Values)
    -       if !ok {
    -           return stdLogger()
    5       }
    -
    -       if vals.Logger == nil {
    -           panic(fmt.Sprintf("no logger in %#v", vals))
    -       }
    10      return vals.Logger
    -   }
    -
    -   // stdLogger returns a logger that behaves like the top-level function in
    -   // the log package
    15  func stdLogger() *log.Logger {
    -       return log.New(log.Writer(), log.Prefix(), log.Flags())
    -   }
```

Now you can use these functions in an HTTP handler. First, create the top-level context for this request:

concurrency/ctx_log/ctx_log.go
```
timeout := 100 * time.Millisecond
ctx, cancel := context.WithTimeout(context.Background(), timeout)
defer cancel()
```

Then you generate a new identifier for the request and create a logger:

concurrency/ctx_log/ctx_log.go
```
id := newID()
logger := idLogger(id)
logger.Printf("info: usersHandler: id=%s", id)
```

Finally, add the logger to the context:

concurrency/ctx_log/ctx_log.go
```
values := Values{
    RequestID: id,
    Logger:    logger,
}
ctx = context.WithValue(ctx, valuesKey, &values)
users, err := getAllUsers(ctx)
```

From here, lower-level functions, such as getAllUsers, that accept a context can use ctxLogger to extract the logger and use it.

To test it out, you issue a call to /users and then look at the logs:

```
<cj3sru2b72acpr009je0> 2023/07/31 18:06:32 info: usersHandler: \
    id=cj3sru2b72acpr009je0
<cj3sru2b72acpr009je0> 2023/07/31 18:06:32 info: getting all users
<cj3sru2b72acpr009je0> 2023/07/31 18:06:32 info: usersHandler: got 0 users
```

Discussion

If you've ever worked with threads, you might be familiar with *thread local storage*.

Variables in thread local storage are unique to the current thread and are shared among all the functions running in this thread. Go does not have a "goroutine-level" storage (like thread local storage in other languages); you need to pass a context around to all the functions that you want to share the same information with.

I've seen context used to pass loggers, authenticated users, shared resources, and many other types of parameters. If you won't use the context storage, you'll have to add a parameter for each piece of information you want to pass down the line. The decision of what should be a function parameter and what should come in a context isn't an easy one. Personally, I try to pass most of the information a function requires as a parameter.

To avoid collision with other packages storing values in the context, you define your own ctxKey type. This way, even if you and another package use the same key name, it'll be stored as a different key.

Since the context uses any for keys and values, you'll need to use a type assertion to convert the value from any to the desired type. In our case, we use a type assertion in line 2 to convert the value to a *log.Logger. Since type assertion might panic, we use the comma, ok paradigm to check that there's a *logger.Logger under the loggerKey.

Added request information to the logs is very helpful. If you want to store more than just the request identifier in the logs, I recommend logging all the extra information *once* with the request identifier; from then on log only the request identifier.

If you need to pass more than one value in the context, a good practice is to use a struct that holds all of these values and have a single entry in the context. Going one step further, you can store a *pointer* to this struct, and then downstream function calls can propagate information up using the context as well.

Final Thoughts

Concurrency is never easy, but Go makes it more accessible for developers. Goroutines and channels take some time to get used to, but once you do, you'll find them simple to work with.

Next, we'll look at Go's lower-level concurrency primitives.

## CHAPTER 10

Lower-Level Concurrency

Go encourages you to use goroutines and channels for concurrency. But in some cases, other forms of coordination and synchronization will be a better fit.

In this chapter, we'll look at the sync and sync/atomic packages, which provide lower-level concurrency primitives. These primitives, such as sync.Mutex, can be used to synchronize access to shared resources or coordinate goroutines.

Finally, the even-lower-level sync/atomic package provides lower-level synchronization primitives, which are harder to use but are much faster than both sync primitives and channels.

Recipe 52

Writing Idempotent Functions with sync.Once

Task

You are tasked with implementing the web server configuration system. The operations team is following "the twelve-factor app"[1] methodology and want to use a configuration system that's based on environment variables.

During a design session, Doug, one of the senior engineers, says, "Make sure loading the configuration is idempotent." You say: "Sure ... what does idempotent mean?" From there the design session derails into topics in mathematics and functional programming.

---

1. https://12factor.net/

In short, an idempotent operation is one that can be applied several times without changing the result of the initial application. For example, say you have On and Off buttons—pressing On more than one time won't change the state of the machine.

What the senior engineer meant was that you should load the configuration only once. Once the configuration is loaded, every call to the function that loads the configuration should do nothing.

Before you part, Doug says, "We like to have environment variables prefixed (say, HTTPD_), but make the prefix configurable."

Solution

First you define the configuration struct and a sync.Once variable:

concurrency/sync/config/config.go
```
var (
    cfgOnce sync.Once
    Config  struct {
        ListenAddress string
        Verbose       bool
    }
)
```

Then you write a loadConfig function to read the configuration from the environment:

concurrency/sync/config/config.go
```
func loadConfig(envPrefix string) {
    // Utility function to get from environment with prefix
    getEnv := func(name string) string {
        key := fmt.Sprintf("%s_%s", envPrefix, name)
        return os.Getenv(key)
    }

    addr := getEnv("ADDRESS")
    if len(addr) == 0 { // default
        Config.ListenAddress = ":8080"
    } else {
        Config.ListenAddress = addr
    }
    verbose := getEnv("VERBOSE")
    if verbose == "1" || verbose == "yes" || verbose == "on" {
        Config.Verbose = true
    }
    log.Printf("configuration loaded (prefix=%s): %+v", envPrefix, Config)
}
```

And finally, you write an exported LoadConfig function:

```
concurrency/sync/config/config.go
// LoadConfig loads configuration once from environment.
func LoadConfig(envPrefix string) {
    cfgOnce.Do(func() {
        loadConfig(envPrefix)
    })
}
```

Discussion

At first, you might think about using a Boolean variable to know if the configuration was loaded or not. But remember that goroutines might be involved, and you'll also need a mutex to guard this flag.

The Do operation of sync.Once guarantees that loadConfig will be called only once.

Unlike Go's defer and go keyword that except a function call, sync.Once.Do excepts a function without arguments. You use an anonymous function to pass the environment prefix.

I've found sync.Once handy in several situations. Most of the time, the underlying reason was the same—idempotency. This recipe is about configuration, but you can also use sync.Once to make sure payments are not processed twice or that users are notified only once.

Recipe 53

Waiting for Job Completion with sync.WaitGroup

Task

Your startup is writing the next great chat system that will be used by everyone and will finally bring IRC down!

Tamar, your team lead, asks you to implement the mechanism that broadcasts messages to all connected clients in a chat room. In the issue, she also writes:

> We don't like to run notifications sequentially since if we have a slow connection, it'll slow down notifications to all other clients. Please notify all clients concurrently, but the act of notification should wait until all clients are notified.

Solution

You start with a simple definition of a room that holds a slice of clients:

concurrency/sync/chat/chat.go
```
// Room is a chat room.
type Room struct {
    clients []io.Writer
}
```

Next, you want to write a Notify function that will send a message to all clients connected to the room in parallel:

concurrency/sync/chat/chat.go
```
// Notify sends msg to all clients in parallel.
// It will return after all messages are sent.
func (r *Room) Notify(msg string) {
    var wg sync.WaitGroup

    wg.Add(len(r.clients))
    for _, c := range r.clients {
        go func(w io.Writer) {
            defer wg.Done()
            w.Write([]byte(msg))
        }(c)
    }
    wg.Wait()
}
```

To test, you create a test Client that saves messages to a common sink:

concurrency/sync/chat/chat_test.go
```
type Sink struct {
    mu       sync.Mutex
    messages []string
}

func (s *Sink) Add(message string) {
    s.mu.Lock()
    defer s.mu.Unlock()
    s.messages = append(s.messages, message)
}

type Client struct {
    id   int
    sink *Sink
}
```

```go
// Write implements io.Writer
func (c *Client) Write(data []byte) (int, error) {
    c.sink.Add(string(data))
    return len(data), nil
}
```

And then you write a test:

concurrency/sync/chat/chat_test.go
```go
func TestNotify(t *testing.T) {
    var s Sink
    var clients []io.Writer
    const n = 3
    for i := 0; i < n; i++ {
        clients = append(clients, &Client{i, &s})
    }
    r := Room{clients}
    msg := "Who's on first?"
    r.Notify(msg)
    require.Equal(t, n, len(s.messages))
    for _, m := range s.messages {
        require.Equal(t, msg, m)
    }
}
```

Discussion

You start a goroutine per client and would like to wait for all of them to finish before returning from the Notify function.

sync.WaitGroup was created exactly for these scenarios when you need to wait for a group of goroutines to finish before moving on. sync.WaitGroup has an internal counter that is increased with its Add method. The Done method decreases the sync.WaitGroup counter by one. When you call the Wait method, you will be blocked until the internal counter reaches zero, which means that all workers are done.

It's a good practice to call Done in a defer. This guarantees that Done will be called even if there was a panic in the worker goroutine, thus preventing a deadlock.

wg.Wait does not return any value, which is good if you only need to know that all workers are done. If you need to get errors as well, have a look at golang.org/x/sync/errgroup, which does that and more.

Recipe 54

Allowing Multiple Readers with sync.RWMutex

Task

When you come back from lunch, you see that Amir, your team lead, assigned a new issue to you:

> We'd like to support dynamic change of configuration. For example, we'd like to set log level to DEBUG in production and then dial it back to INFO an hour later. We know that a lock will be involved, but try not to hurt the performance of reading the configuration too much.

You read the sync package documentation and then start to code.

Solution

You define the configuration as a map[string]string and use a sync.RWMutex to guard it:

concurrency/sync/dyn_conf/dyn_conf.go
```
var (
    cfgLock sync.RWMutex
    config  = make(map[string]string)
)
```

You allow multiple readers at the same time by using RLock:

concurrency/sync/dyn_conf/dyn_conf.go
```
// GetConfig returns the value for key in configuration.
func GetConfig(key string) string {
    cfgLock.RLock()
    defer cfgLock.RUnlock()

    return config[key]
}
```

And you provide a single writer that updates the configuration with Lock:

concurrency/sync/dyn_conf/dyn_conf.go
```
// ReloadConfig reloads configuration.
func ReloadConfig() {
    cfgLock.Lock()
    defer cfgLock.Unlock()

    config["updated"] = time.Now().String()
    // TODO: finish loading configuration
}
```

Discussion

The built-in data structures, such as map and slice, are not safe for access and modify from different goroutines. This is a design decision most programming languages have—adding locks creates cost in performance.

sync.RWMutex will allow only one writer with no readers or many readers with no writer.

You *can* use a regular sync.Mutex, but then only one reader at a time will be able to access the configuration. This is not an optimal use of the concurrency Go offers.

Dynamic Configuration

Changing configuration in a running application is risky. Consider what happens when you load the new configuration and encounter an error: can you revert to the old configuration? Or will you continue to run with inconsistent configuration?

I highly recommend restarting your application when the configuration changes and validating the configuration after loading it. It'll save you a lot of grief in the future.

| Recipe 55 |

Using the Race Detector

Task

Aditi from operations comes over and says, "We think that the metrics your server is showing are wrong. I hit an endpoint 1,000 times and saw only 987 in the metric."

You ask her to create an issue and assign it to you. Next morning, the issue waits for you with high priority, and you start working on it.

Solution

You start by looking at the code, and then you create a simple program that mimics what the code does.

You create a single metric, called callCount:

concurrency/counter/counter.go
```
var (
    callCount int
)
```

You then create a simple handler that increments the counter and sleeps for a random time:

concurrency/counter/counter.go
```
func handler(w http.ResponseWriter, r *http.Request) {
    callCount++
    // Simulate work
    time.Sleep(time.Duration(rand.Intn(100)) * time.Microsecond)
    w.Write([]byte("OK"))
}
```

And then, in main, you run several goroutines that call the handler:

concurrency/counter/counter.go
```
const nRuns = 1000
const nGoroutines = 10

var wg sync.WaitGroup
wg.Add(nGoroutines)
for g := 0; g < nGoroutines; g++ {
    go func() {
        defer wg.Done()
        for i := 0; i < nRuns; i++ {
            // Dummy ResponseWriter & http.Request for the handler
            w := httptest.NewRecorder()
            r := httptest.NewRequest("GET", "localhost:8080", nil)
            handler(w, r)
        }
    }()
}
```

Finally, wait for the goroutines to finish and print out the value of callCount:

concurrency/counter/counter.go
```
wg.Wait()
fmt.Println(callCount)
```

However, when you run the code, you see this:

```
$ go run counter.go
sleeping for 20s
9914
```

Oops!

Different Results

You'll probably see a different number when you run the code. Concurrency issues are unpredictable and hard to reproduce.

You figure there's probably a race condition and reach out for the race detector.[2]

```
$ go run -race counter.go
==================
WARNING: DATA RACE
Read at 0x0000007e2e78 by goroutine 12:
  main.handler()
.../counter/counter/counter.go:21 +0x37
  main.main.func1()
.../counter/counter/counter.go:43 +0xee

Previous write at 0x0000007e2e78 by goroutine 15:
  main.handler()
.../counter/counter/counter.go:21 +0x4f
  main.main.func1()
.../counter/counter/counter.go:43 +0xee

Goroutine 12 (running) created at:
  main.main()
.../counter/counter/counter.go:37 +0x6d

Goroutine 15 (running) created at:
  main.main()
.../counter/counter/counter.go:37 +0x6d
==================
==================
WARNING: DATA RACE
Write at 0x0000007e2e78 by goroutine 11:
  main.handler()
.../counter/counter/counter.go:21 +0x4f
  main.main.func1()
.../counter/counter/counter.go:43 +0xee

Previous write at 0x0000007e2e78 by goroutine 12:
  main.handler()
.../counter/counter/counter.go:21 +0x4f
  main.main.func1()
.../counter/counter/counter.go:43 +0xee

Goroutine 11 (running) created at:
  main.main()
.../counter/counter/counter.go:37 +0x6d
```

---

2. https://go.dev/doc/articles/race_detector

```
Goroutine 12 (running) created at:
  main.main()
.../counter/counter/counter.go:37 +0x6d
===================
6721
Found 2 data race(s)
exit status 66
```

You start by changing the type of callCount to int64:

concurrency/counter/fix/counter.go
```
var (
    callCount int64
)
```

Then in the handler, use atomic.AddInt64 instead of the ++ operator:

concurrency/counter/fix/counter.go
```
func handler(w http.ResponseWriter, r *http.Request) {
    atomic.AddInt64(&callCount, 1)

    // Simulate work
    time.Sleep(time.Duration(rand.Intn(100)) * time.Microsecond)
    w.Write([]byte("OK"))
}
```

Now when you run the code, you see the expected result:

```
$ go run -race counter.go
10000
```

Discussion

The reason for the bug is modern computers usually have three layers of cache before accessing the main memory, as you can see in the following image:

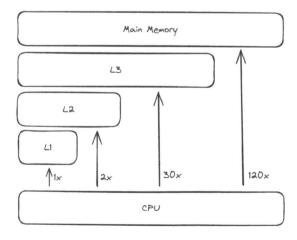

Accessing the cache is faster, but it means that every goroutine might see a different value of callCount, depending on the cache and memory ordering.

Reading and writing a value from different goroutines is known as a *race condition*. You can use the go tool -race flag to catch these issues.

To solve this issue, we need a memory barrier[3] that will make sure all goroutines see the same value of callCount. We can use a sync.Mutex, but since you're performance-oriented, use atomic.AddInt64.

The int type is an alias for the native integer type of your machine. When working with atomic operations, we need to be specific about the types we use—int64 in our case.

How much faster is atomic.AddInt64 than sync.Mutex? Let's write a benchmark to see:

concurrency/counter/bench_test.go
```go
package main

import (
    "sync"
    "sync/atomic"
    "testing"
)

var (
    count int64
    m     sync.Mutex
)

func BenchmarkMutex(b *testing.B) {
    for i := 0; i < b.N; i++ {
        m.Lock()
        count++
        m.Unlock()
    }
}

func BenchmarkAtomic(b *testing.B) {
    for i := 0; i < b.N; i++ {
        atomic.AddInt64(&count, 1)
    }
}
```

And now run it:

---

3.   https://www.kernel.org/doc/Documentation/memory-barriers.txt

```
$ go test -bench . bench_test.go
goos: linux
goarch: amd64
cpu: 12th Gen Intel(R) Core(TM) i7-1255U
BenchmarkMutex-12        44517554              25.59 ns/op
BenchmarkAtomic-12      144230883               8.343 ns/op
PASS
ok      command-line-arguments  3.218s
```

It's about twice as fast. Note that Lock/Unlock is about fifteen nanoseconds—which should be more than fast enough for most applications.

Using sync/atomic is usually a code smell since it's very low level. You should rethink and use higher-level synchronization primitives. Unless you have very tight performance restrictions, try to use channels or the sync package.

For metrics, use the built-in expvar package (see *Using Metrics as Eyes to Production*) or external systems such as Prometheus.

Recipe 56

Using sync/atomic for a Faster Now

Task

You're writing a very performance-sensitive HTTP server. To find out where to spend your next optimization effort, you run a profiler on your code.

You see that the main candidate for optimization is the logging. Digging further, you see that every time you log, you record the current time using time.Now. Compared to the rest of the logging code, time.Now takes most of the computation time.

Slow Logging

 I get called to help with optimization problems for various clients. The first thing I do is turn off logging. Sometimes, it's all I need to do.

You talk with Ivan over lunch, and together you have a plan.

Solution

You start by defining a now variable:

concurrency/now/now.go
```go
var (
    now atomic.Value
)
```

Next, in init, you start a goroutine that will update now periodically:

concurrency/now/now.go
```go
func init() {
    now.Store(time.Now())
    go func() {
        for {
            time.Sleep(time.Millisecond)
            now.Store(time.Now())
        }
    }()
}
```

And finally, you provide a Now function:

concurrency/now/now.go
```go
// Now return the current time in 1ms granularily
func Now() time.Time {
    return now.Load().(time.Time)
}
```

To validate, you create a benchmark to compare the two versions of now:

concurrency/now/bench_test.go
```go
package httpd

import (
    "testing"
    "time"
)

var (
    t time.Time
)

func BenchmarkTimeNow(b *testing.B) {
    for i := 0; i < b.N; i++ {
        t = time.Now()
    }
}

func BenchmarkNow(b *testing.B) {
    for i := 0; i < b.N; i++ {
        t = Now()
    }
}
```

And run it:

```
go test -bench .
goos: linux
goarch: amd64
pkg: github.com/353solutions/go-cookbook/concurrency/now
cpu: 12th Gen Intel(R) Core(TM) i7-1255U
BenchmarkTimeNow-12        22844953                    49.34 ns/op
BenchmarkNow-12            523512082                    2.310 ns/op
...
```

Your Now is about twenty-one times faster than the built-in time.Now—not bad for about thirty-five lines of code.

Benchmark Results

 If you run this benchmark on your machine, you'll see different results. Benchmarks depend on the hardware, operating system, load, and many more factors.

Discussion

sync/atomic has a Value type. This type can be used to store and get values in a goroutine-safe way *without using a lock*, which makes it ideal for performance-critical code.

In Now, you use the Load method of now and convert the result, which is any to time.Time:

The accuracy of your Now function will be less than the time.Now, but it'll be much faster. You'll always have trade-offs!

Final Thoughts

Working with the lower-level concurrency primitives requires a lot of thought and care. Many edge cases are not caught during testing, and debugging concurrency bugs in production is very hard. My advice is that unless you have a good reason, stay with goroutines and channels.

Next, we'll look at another lower-level technology—sockets.

## CHAPTER 11

Working with Sockets

Sockets are one of the basic building blocks of communication. When two programs want to communicate, either on the same machine or on different machines, most of the time they'll use sockets.

The net package contains code for working with all kinds of sockets. What's nice is that sockets implement io.Reader and io.Writer, so you can use many standard functions and types with them.

Recipe 57

Accepting Files over TCP Sockets

Task

The SRE team designed a system where logs are shipped to a central server via agents. After several design sessions, the team decided not to use a known protocol such as HTTP but instead to transfer files over TCP sockets.

The task of writing a proof-of-concept server and client falls on you.

Since sockets only pass bytes from one side to another, you start by designing the message format. You decide on a simple format with a header containing the file size, space, the file name, and another space—like this, for example:

```
2020-01-01-httpd.log 137383
```

After the header, you'll send the content of the file. The server will reply with a single line of status.

Solution

You start by listening on a TCP socket:

sockets/logs/server/server.go
```
addr := ":8765"
ln, err := net.Listen("tcp", addr)
if err != nil {
    log.Fatalf("error: %s", err)
}

log.Printf("server ready on %s", addr)
```

Then you run an infinite loop that accepts a connection and then starts a handler goroutine:

sockets/logs/server/server.go
```
for {
    c, err := ln.Accept()
    if err != nil {
        log.Fatalf("error: %s", err)
    }
    log.Printf("new connection from %s", c.RemoteAddr())
    go fileHandler(c)
}
```

The handler function starts by making sure it closes the connection:

sockets/logs/server/server.go
```
func fileHandler(c net.Conn) {
    defer c.Close()
```

Then it reads the header line:

sockets/logs/server/server.go
```
var fileName string
var size int64
if _, err := fmt.Fscanf(c, "%s %d", &fileName, &size); err != nil {
    log.Printf("can't read file size: %s", err)
    fmt.Fprintf(c, "error: %s\n", err)
    return
}
log.Printf("%s: %d", fileName, size)

if size > maxSize {
    log.Printf("size %d > %d", size, maxSize)
    fmt.Fprintf(c, "error: size %d > %d\n", size, maxSize)
    return
}
```

Once you have the file name and size, you can copy size bytes from the socket to the destination file:

sockets/logs/server/server.go
```
// Save in "logs" directory
fileName = path.Join("logs", strings.TrimSpace(fileName))
log.Printf("fileName: %s", fileName)

file, err := os.Create(fileName)
if err != nil {
    log.Printf("can't open %s - %s", fileName, err)
    fmt.Fprintf(c, "error: %s\n", err)
    return
}
defer file.Close()

n, err := io.CopyN(file, c, size)
if err != nil {
    log.Printf("can't copy to %s: %s", fileName, err)
    fmt.Fprintf(c, "error: %s\n", err)
    return
}

if n != size {
    log.Printf("got %d bytes of %d", n, size)
    fmt.Fprintf(c, "error: %d of %d bytes", n, size)
    return
}
```

And finally, you send an "OK" message back to the client.

sockets/logs/server/server.go
```
fmt.Fprintf(c, "ok: %d bytes written to %s\n", n, fileName)
```

To try it out, you run the server and then use nc to send data to the server:

```
$ echo 'pi.txt 4 3.14' | nc localhost 8765
ok: 4 bytes written to logs/pi.txt
read(net): Connection reset by peer
$ cat /logs/pi.txt
3.14%
```

The Connection reset by peer message is due to the server closing the connection, and the % at the end of the file means there's no newline.

Discussion

Once you start working at the TCP level, you'll need to do a lot of things yourself—design a protocol, check for errors, and more. If you use HTTP for the same functionality, the code will be much shorter.

We designed a simple protocol. You might want to add a digital signature for the file, as well, to detect transport errors. Spend time thinking about the protocol, make it simple, and if possible, use existing serialization formats, such as JSON.

The infinite server loop is typical to servers. Servers are meant to run forever or until you terminate them, typically for a version update or a bug fix.

Go makes it easy to add concurrency—run each handler in a goroutine.

Both sockets and files implement both io.Reader and io.Writer, which allows you to use functions such as fmt.Fscanf and io.Copy.

Recipe 58

Sending Files over TCP Sockets

Task

After you finish, it's time to go home. Next morning, you start working on the client. The client will get the server address and a file name, which it needs to send to the server.

Solution

You write sendFile, which gets the server address and the file to send:

sockets/logs/client/client.go
```go
func sendFile(addr, fileName string) error {
```

First, you connect to the server using the net.Dial function:

sockets/logs/client/client.go
```go
c, err := net.Dial("tcp", addr)
if err != nil {
    return err
}
defer c.Close()
```

Next, you open the file and find out its size:

sockets/logs/client/client.go
```go
file, err := os.Open(fileName)
if err != nil {
    return err
}
```

```
defer file.Close()
info, err := file.Stat()
if err != nil {
    return err
}
```

Now you can start sending data. First is the header line with the size and the file name:

sockets/logs/client/client.go
```
// Send header line with file size & name
_, err = fmt.Fprintf(c, "%s %d ", fileName, info.Size())
if err != nil {
    return err
}
```

And then you send the content of the file:

sockets/logs/client/client.go
```
// Send file content
_, err = io.Copy(c, file)
if err != nil {
    return err
}
```

Finally, you read the reply from the server:

sockets/logs/client/client.go
```
const maxReply = 1 << 10 // 1KB
data, err := io.ReadAll(io.LimitReader(c, maxReply))
if err != nil {
    return err
}

reply := string(data)
log.Printf("reply: %s", reply)
if strings.HasPrefix(reply, "error") {
    return fmt.Errorf(reply)
}

return nil
```

You write some code to test by sending the client source file to the server:

sockets/logs/client/client.go
```
func main() {
    if err := sendFile("localhost:8765", "client.go"); err != nil {
        log.Fatalf("error: %s", err)
    }
}
```

Now you can try it out:

```
$ go run client.go
2023/08/01 15:45:24 reply: ok: 1163 bytes written to logs/client.go
$ diff ../server/logs/client.go client.go
```

No output from diff means the files are equal.

Discussion

net.Dial can work with several protocols, such as "tcp", "udp", "unix", and others. It returns a net.Conn, which is an interface with common methods to all underlying sockets. If you want a specific connection type, you can use type assertion:

```
tc, ok := c.(*net.TCPConn)
if ok {
    // SetKeepAlive is specific to TCPConn
    tc.SetKeepAlive(true)
}
```

net.Conn implements io.Writer, and our opened file implements io.Reader. We use fmt.Fprint to construct the header line and io.Copy to copy the file.

Recipe 59

Writing a Serverless Platform

Task

Your company has servers sending events and would like teams to have the freedom to write process-handling code in several languages. To separate the consumption of events from the code processing them, you're writing a serverless platform.

After a design session, you write the following issue:

> Every RPC call involves:
>
> - Marshaling/serializing a message to a sequence of bytes
> - Calling a remote server via a communication medium
> - Unmarshaling the result from a sequence of bytes

Since we want to support a wide variety of programming languages, we'll use JSON as the serialization format. For the communication medium, we'll be using Unix domain sockets.

Solution

You start with a function to process messages. These messages come from a channel. You also get the connection to the server handling the connections:

sockets/rpc/rpc.go
```go
func processMessages(conn io.ReadWriteCloser, ch <-chan Message) error {
```

First you create input and output objects to call and receive messages:

sockets/rpc/rpc.go
```go
dec := json.NewDecoder(conn)
enc := json.NewEncoder(conn)
```

enc handles both the marshaling of messages and sending them over the socket. r allows you to read one line at a time.

Then you start a for loop on the channel:

sockets/rpc/rpc.go
```go
for msg := range ch {
```

First, you encode and send the message:

sockets/rpc/rpc.go
```go
// json encoder add newline
if err := enc.Encode(msg); err != nil {
    return err
}
```

Then you read the output line, decode it, and print a log of the result.

sockets/rpc/rpc.go
```go
var reply struct {
    Output any
}
if err := dec.Decode(&reply); err != nil {
    return err
}
log.Printf("%#v -> %#v", msg, reply.Output)
```

Once you have this code in place, you write some testing code. You start the server first:

```
sockets/rpc/rpc.go
cmd := exec.Command(
    "go", "run", "server/main.go",
    "-socket", socketFile,
)
cmd.Stdout = os.Stdout
cmd.Stderr = os.Stderr
if err := cmd.Start(); err != nil {
    log.Fatalf("error: %s", err)
}
defer cmd.Process.Kill()

time.Sleep(time.Second) // Give server time to load (FIXME: timeout)
```

Then you connect to the Unix domain socket:

```
sockets/rpc/rpc.go
sock, err := net.Dial("unix", socketFile)
if err != nil {
    log.Fatalf("error: %s", err)
}
defer sock.Close()
```

And finally, you create a channel, populate it with a message, and run processMessages with the channel and the connection:

```
sockets/rpc/rpc.go
ch := make(chan Message)
go func() {
    ch <- Message{Text: "Was it a cat I saw?"}
    close(ch)
}()

if err := processMessages(sock, ch); err != nil {
    log.Fatalf("error: %s", err)
}
```

Running this code prints the following:

```
server: 2022/05/08 16:36:37 deleting "/tmp/srv.sock"
server: 2022/05/08 16:36:37 server running on "/tmp/srv.sock"
2022/05/08 16:36:38 main.Message{Text:"Was it a cat I saw?"} -> \
    "?was I tac a ti saW"
```

The first two log messages are from the server, and the last one is from our client.

Discussion

RPC calls or handlers are defined by two technology choices: the marshaling/serialization format and the transport medium. The serialization format can be JSON, protocol buffers, XML, and many others. The transport can be HTTP, sockets, pipes, and others.

Most of the time, once you pick an RPC framework, such as gRPC, these decisions are made for you. If you have the option to pick an RPC framework, think about what fits your needs more. For example, JSON is supported by many languages but has a very limited set of types it supports. For instance, you can't natively send time.Time using it.

Your code is very minimal, and there's much to improve on:

- Improve error handling
- Add timeout on calls
- Detect and handle server crashes
- Support streaming of messages

A mature RPC framework will solve all of the above problems and more.

If you're working in Go and calling functions in the same process, there's no need to use RPC. Only use it if you're calling across processes, machines or if you want to support several programming languages (did someone say "microservices"?).

Recipe 60

Reading Time with NTP over UDP

Task

Your team found out that the application server clock is drifting from the actual time. Due to the drift, logs have the wrong timestamp, which makes it hard to order them and debug issues.

Emma, your team lead, tasks you with updating the current time in the application from a network time protocol[1](NTP) server.

---

ntdp

 This problem can (and should) be solved with running a service like ntpd server.[2] I'm using this recipe as an example for using UDP, not synchronizing time.

---

1. https://www.ntp.org/documentation/4.2.8-series/
2. https://linux.die.net/man/8/ntpd

Solution

You read RFC5905[3] and find out that NTP is a binary protocol over UDP. You start by writing an NTPMessage struct according to the NTP spec:

sockets/ntp/ntp.go
```
// NTPMessage is an NTP message.
type NTPMessage struct {
    VNMode              uint8
    Stratum             uint8
    Poll                uint8
    Precision           uint8
    RootDelay           uint32
    RootDispersion      uint32
    RefID               uint32
    RefTimeSec          uint32
    RefTimeFrac         uint32
    OrigTimeSec         uint32
    OrigTimeFrac        uint32
    ReceivedTimeSec     uint32
    ReceivedTimeFrac    uint32
    TransmitTimeSec     uint32
    TransmitTimeFrac    uint32
}
```

Then you read in the NTP spec that its epoch (0) time is January 1, 1900, whereas Go (and most languages) uses January 1, 1970, as epoch. If you want to read more about epoch, head over to Discussion, on page 101.

You write a function to calculate this difference:

sockets/ntp/ntp.go
```
func ntpDelta() time.Duration {
    unixEpoch := time.Date(1970, 1, 1, 0, 0, 0, 0, time.UTC)
    ntpEpoch := time.Date(1900, 1, 1, 0, 0, 0, 0, time.UTC)
    return ntpEpoch.Sub(unixEpoch)
}
```

Since you need to calculate this difference only once, you create a global variable holding this value:

sockets/ntp/ntp.go
```
var (
    NTPDelta = ntpDelta()
    zeroTime time.Time
)
```

---

3. https://datatracker.ietf.org/doc/html/rfc5905

You also create a global variable for the zero time, to be returned in case of errors.

To calculate time from an NTPMessage, you add a TransmitTime method to it:

```
sockets/ntp/ntp.go
// TransmitTime returns the transmit time.
func (n *NTPMessage) TransmitTime() time.Time {
    secs := int64(n.TransmitTimeSec)
    nanos := (int64(n.TransmitTimeFrac) * 1e9) >> 32
    return time.Unix(secs, nanos).Add(NTPDelta)
}
```

Now you can start writing CurrentTime, which gets the address of an NTP host and creates a UDP connection to it:

```
sockets/ntp/ntp.go
// CurrentTime returns the current time from NTP host.
func CurrentTime(addr string) (time.Time, error) {
    conn, err := net.Dial("udp", addr)
    if err != nil {
        return zeroTime, err
    }
    defer conn.Close()
```

Then you create a message and initialize it:

```
sockets/ntp/ntp.go
msg := NTPMessage{
    VNMode: 0b00011011, // li = 0, vn = 3, and mode = 3
}
```

Next, you encode and send the message using encoding/binary:

```
sockets/ntp/ntp.go
if err := binary.Write(conn, binary.BigEndian, msg); err != nil {
    return zeroTime, err
}
```

Now you read back the message from the server and decode it:

```
sockets/ntp/ntp.go
if err := binary.Read(conn, binary.BigEndian, &msg); err != nil {
    return zeroTime, err
}
```

And finally, you return the time sent by the server:

```
sockets/ntp/ntp.go
return msg.TransmitTime(), nil
```

Discussion

UDP does not have guarantees on transmissions like TCP. It's faster but sometimes needs more logic to verify that messages were received by the other side and in order.

Sometimes you'll use UDP since it's the standard, like NTP and UDP. In other cases, you might consider UDP since it's faster or can do broadcasts.

HTTP/3

 Currently, the HTTP protocol uses TCP sockets. The next version, HTTP/3 will use UDP sockets.

Once you create a UDP connection, you can work with the familiar io.Reader and io.Writer again.

You use io.Copy and binary.Read over the connection.

Most of the code is a bit of twiddling and time calculations, which is typical of low-level networking code. Once you shuffle bits a couple of times, you'll get the hang of it.

Final Thoughts

Our code is riddled with error checking, even more than usual for Go. Working with sockets feels, and is, lower level than working with HTTP, gRPC, and other methods. If you have a choice, pick a high-level established protocol—it'll save you a lot of work. But in some cases, mostly when you need the extra performance, you can consider working with sockets.

The nice thing about Go is that it makes working with sockets easy. Once you establish a connection, you switch to working with io.Reader and io.Writer—a lot of built-in functions accept them.

L. Peter Deutsch and others at Sun Microsystems wrote a list of false assumptions, called "Fallacies of distributed computing":

1. The network is reliable
2. Latency is zero
3. Bandwidth is infinite
4. The network is secure
5. Topology doesn't change
6. There is one administrator
7. Transport cost is zero
8. The network is homogeneous

When working with sockets, pay attention to these fallacies. For example, thinking about "the network is secure" fallacy prompted me to limit the number of bytes I read from a socket using an io.LimitReader.

Next, we'll see how you can communicate with non-Go code by either calling executables or importing C libraries.

## CHAPTER 12

Communicating with Non-Go Code

Sadly, not everyone writes in Go.

In many cases, it makes more sense to use existing code from Go than to rewrite the same functionality in Go. For example, the Go bindings to the deep learning library TensorFlow use the underlying C++ library instead of rewriting all the functionality from scratch.

Go has cgo, which makes calling C code relatively easy. But as Rob Pike says, "Cgo is not Go." Once you start using cgo, you lose a lot of things you came to take for granted in Go: cross platform, fast compilation times, automatic memory management, and more. You also need a C compiler on your machine and to know some C.

In this chapter, we'll go over some of the finer points of using cgo. We'll navigate the C jungle and see where the lions sleep.

At one point or another, you'll need to run an external command from your Go code. Most of the time, it's to use something that's already written and working instead of re-implementing it on your own. For example, instead of implementing your own SSH client to copy files over SSH, you can use the scp command.

The built-in os/exec package provides a mechanism to run external commands. You can check command exit status, capture its output, change its environment, and much more. In this chapter, we'll also explore ways to use os/exec.

Recipe 61

Using os/exec to Ping Servers

Task

As part of the SRE team, you have services you can connect to. The developers would like to connect to the one that has the best response time.

Ren, your team lead, says, "Let's start with running ping on the servers and picking the fastest one. Please use median time and not average." You agree and start looking into the problem.

You run ping three times against the pragprog.com server.

```
$ ping -c 3 pragprog.com
PING pragprog.com (161.35.125.80) 56(84) bytes of data.
64 bytes from pragprog.com (161.35.125.80): icmp_seq=1 ttl=51 time=144 ms
64 bytes from pragprog.com (161.35.125.80): icmp_seq=2 ttl=51 time=143 ms
64 bytes from pragprog.com (161.35.125.80): icmp_seq=3 ttl=51 time=142 ms

--- pragprog.com ping statistics ---
3 packets transmitted, 3 received, 0% packet loss, time 2002ms
rtt min/avg/max/mdev = 142.039/142.792/143.503/0.598 ms
```

Ping Time

 Yes, my network is slow—I'm also across the ocean. You will see different, much likely better, ping times.

Solution

Before writing the code to run ping and parse its output, you need to create some utility functions.

The first is a function to calculate median:

nongo/exec/ping_time/ping_time.go
```go
func median(values []float64) float64 {
    // Don't mutate original values
    nums := make([]float64, len(values))
    copy(nums, values)
    sort.Float64s(nums)

    i := len(nums) / 2
```

```
    if len(nums)%2 == 0 {
        return (nums[i-1] + nums[i]) / 2.0
    }

    return nums[i]
}
```

Then you need another function to parse a ping output line and return the time portion as a float64:

nongo/exec/ping_time/ping_time.go
```
// findTime finds the ping time in ping output line
// returns value, found and error
func findTime(line []byte) (float64, bool, error) {
    // 64 bytes from ...: icmp_seq=1 ttl=51 time=142 ms
    var prefix = []byte("time=")
    start := bytes.Index(line, prefix)
    if start == -1 {
        return 0, false, nil
    }
    start += len(prefix) // skip over "time="
    end := bytes.IndexByte(line[start:], ' ')
    if end == -1 {
        return 0, false, fmt.Errorf("can't find end")
    }

    end += start
    val, err := strconv.ParseFloat(string(line[start:end]), 64)
    if err != nil {
        return 0, false, err
    }

    return val, true, nil
}
```

Now you're ready to write your function:

nongo/exec/ping_time/ping_time.go
```
Line 1  // medianPing returns the median time of <count> pings to <host>.
   -    func medianPingTime(host string, count int) (float64, error) {
   -        sw := "-c"
   -        if runtime.GOOS == "windows" {
   5            sw = "-n" // windows ping uses -n for count
   -        }
   -
   -        // ping -c 4 pragprog.com
   -        cmd := exec.Command("ping", sw, fmt.Sprintf("%d", count), host)
  10
   -        data, err := cmd.Output()
   -        if err != nil {              // Wait for ping to finish
   -            return 0, err
   -        }
```

```
15      values := make([]float64, 0, count)
        s := bufio.NewScanner(bytes.NewReader(data))
        for s.Scan() {
            val, found, err := findTime(s.Bytes())
20          if err != nil {
                return 0, err
            }
            if !found {
                continue
25          }
            values = append(values, val)
        }

        if err := s.Err(); err != nil {
30          return 0, err
        }

        return median(values), nil
    }
```

In line 11, you run ping and collect its standard output. Then, in line 17, you iterate over the output using a bufio.Scanner and, finally, calculate the median.

Discussion

You can probably write the portion of ping you need in Go using ICMP. However, ping is pre-installed on most operating systems, and you can use it.

os/exec makes it easy to start a process and read its output. Process output is a []byte, and you need to convert or parse that output into the desired types.

Run will wait for the process to terminate, so it's a good idea to have a timeout on the execution time of Run. Use the CommandContext function in os/exec to implement deadlines and cancellations. See Recipe 50, Using context.Context for Timeouts, on page 143, on how to use context.Context for timeouts.

Recipe 62

Calling C Functions to AlignText

Task

As part of the SRE team, you maintain some command-line utilities that print out information to the screen. This morning, you see the following issue assigned to you:

> The command-line utilities work great. However, I'd like to make the output nicer-looking. It'll make it easier for us humans to read the output and understand what's going on.

After a short discussion, you agree that you'll start by writing headers that are centered on the screen.

Solution

You start looking at how to find the screen width from inside the program. You find the iocl C function that can return the current terminal height and width.

Linux Only

 This code will run on Linux machines only. That's a price you need to pay when using cgo—no more platform-agnostic code.

You write a C function called term_width:

nongo/center/center.go
```
/*
#include <sys/ioctl.h>
#include <stdio.h>
#include <unistd.h>

int term_width() {
    struct winsize w;
    ioctl(STDOUT_FILENO, TIOCGWINSZ, &w);
    return w.ws_col;
}
*/
import "C"
```

The C code is in a comment, and right after it there's an import "C" statement. This tells the go tool to compile the C code using a C compiler and expose this function under the C module.

Now you can use term_width in your Center function:

nongo/center/center.go
```
width := int(C.term_width()) // Convert C.int to Go int
```

The return value from C.term_width is a C.int, so you need to convert it to a Go int since Go sees them as different types.

Next, you calculate the right and left padding:

nongo/center/center.go
```
textLen := utf8.RuneCountInString(text)
lpad := (width - textLen) / 2 // left padding
if lpad <= 0 {                    // text >= screen width
    return text
}
rpad := width - len(text) - lpad // right padding
```

Finally, you construct the new string, using fmt.Sprintf:

nongo/center/center.go
```
return fmt.Sprintf("%*s%s%*s", lpad, " ", text, rpad, " ")
```

And as usual, you write a small test:

nongo/center/center.go
```
func main() {
    fmt.Println(Center("Hello Gophers!"))
}
```

On my terminal, running the code produces Hello Gophers! in the center of the line.

Discussion

You were able to get the terminal width by writing about ten lines of C code. Using this C code from Go was simple—call a function and get a return value.

Note that you'll need a C compiler to build and run the code.

If we use the Linux ldd on the executable, we'll see the following output:

```
$ go build -o center center.go
$ ldd center
    linux-vdso.so.1 (0x00007fffccd5e000)
    libc.so.6 => /usr/lib/libc.so.6 (0x00007fc29b925000)
    /lib64/ld-linux-x86-64.so.2 => /usr/lib64/ld-linux-x86-64.so.2 \
        (0x00007fc29bb38000)
```

You see that our executable is linked to several shared libraries. This means that you need to have these libraries, preferably in the exact same version, on the target machine.

Using cgo also means you need a C compiler on your system, so cross compilation becomes much harder. When using third-party packages, try to find "pure Go" ones that don't use cgo—it'll make your life easier.

Recipe 63

Redirecting Subprocess stdin and stdout to Prototype a Calculator

Task

You're working on the configuration system for your application and see the following issue:

> Users asked to be able to use mathematical expressions in the configuration file. For example, maxSize = 5 * (2^20) # 5MB.

The product teams decided this issue has high priority, and they'd like you to provide a prototype quickly. Currently, the code that parses files returns only strings, and you need to write the code that calculates these values.

Solution

Since production is running on Linux, you decide to use the bc command-line calculator. This will initially save you the work required to parse expressions and evaluate them.

You start by defining a Calc struct:

```
nongo/exec/calc/calc.go
// Calc is a calculator.
type Calc struct {
    p *os.Process  // Underlying process
    w io.Writer    // Process stdin
    r *bufio.Reader // Process stdout & stderr
}
```

Then you write a `NewCalc` function that will start an underlying `bc` process and create pipes to communicate with it:

nongo/exec/calc/calc.go
```
// NewCalc creates a new calculator
func NewCalc() (*Calc, error) {
```

Initially, you create an *exec.Command that will run `bc`:

nongo/exec/calc/calc.go
```
// -l adds mathlib, -q mean no banner
cmd := exec.Command("bc", "-lq")
```

Then you set up pipes to communicate with the underlying process:

nongo/exec/calc/calc.go
```
w, err := cmd.StdinPipe()
if err != nil {
    return nil, err
}

r, err := cmd.StdoutPipe()
if err != nil {
    return nil, err
}
cmd.Stderr = cmd.Stdout // redirect standard error to standard output
```

And at the end of the function, you start the underlying process and return a *Calc struct:

nongo/exec/calc/calc.go
```
if err := cmd.Start(); err != nil {
    return nil, err
}

c := &Calc{
    p: cmd.Process,
    w: w,
    r: bufio.NewReader(r),
}
return c, nil
```

Next comes the `Eval` method, which will send a string to the underlying `bc` process and part the output:

nongo/exec/calc/calc.go
```
// Eval evaluates a math expression such as "3 / 7".
func (c *Calc) Eval(expr string) (float64, error) {
```

First, you send the expression to evaluate to the process:

nongo/exec/calc/calc.go
```go
if _, err := fmt.Fprintf(c.w, "%s\n", expr); err != nil {
    return 0, err
}
```

And then you read back an answer and parse the result, which should be a floating-point number:

nongo/exec/calc/calc.go
```go
line, err := c.r.ReadString('\n')
if err != nil {
    return 0, err
}

line = line[:len(line)-1] // trim \n

val, err := strconv.ParseFloat(line, 64)
if err != nil {
    return 0, err
}

return val, nil
```

Since there's a limit on the number of running processes, you add a Close method that will terminate the underlying bc process:

nongo/exec/calc/calc.go
```go
// Close closes the calculator.
func (c *Calc) Close() error {
    return c.p.Kill()
}
```

And finally, you test your code with some input:

nongo/exec/calc/calc.go
```go
func main() {
    c, err := NewCalc()
    if err != nil {
        log.Fatalf("error: %s", err)
    }
    defer c.Close()

    exprs := []string{
        "7 / 3",
        "sqrt(2)",
        "3/0", // error
        "-4/77",
    }
```

```
for _, expr := range exprs {
    out, err := c.Eval(expr)
    if err != nil {
        fmt.Println(expr, "error:", err)
        continue
    }
    fmt.Println(expr, "→", out)
}
```

Running the program prints the following:

```
7 / 3 → 2.3333333333333335
sqrt(2) → 1.4142135623730951
3/0 error: strconv.ParseFloat: parsing "Runtime error (func=(main), adr=5): \
            Divide by zero": invalid syntax
-4/77 → -0.05194805194805195
```

Discussion

You can communicate with an underlying process by using pipes. These pipes implement io.Reader and io.Writer, which means you can use most of the functions from the standard library with them.

Communicating with a process saves you from starting a new process on every request, but you need to be careful and terminate the underlying process when done.

Recipe 64

Stemming Words Using a C Library

Task

As part of the information team in the company, you're working on a search engine that will help users find documentation and other knowledge in a central location.

Currently, you're working on the following task:

> We need to stem words, both in the index and when a user issues a query. Stemming is the process of converting words to a canonical form. For example, works, worked, and working are all stemmed to work.

Writing a stemmer can take a PhD or two. You don't find a good pure Go stemmer to work with, so you ask Shira, your team lead, if it's OK to use a C-based one. She says, "Sure."

Solution

You decide to use the popular snowball stemmer.

Installing Snowball

You'll need to have snowball and its header files to follow along. Installation procedure depends on your Linux distribution. For the popular Ubuntu Linux distribution, run in a terminal the following command:

```
$ sudo apt-get install -y libstemmer-dev
```

You start by importing the required header files.

nongo/stem/stem.go
```
/*
#include <libstemmer.h>
#include <stdlib.h>

#cgo LDFLAGS: -lstemmer
*/
import "C"
```

You also add a #cgo directive to let the go tool know it needs to link against the libstemmer shared library. If libraries or header files are installed in unconventional locations, the cgo tool knows how to work with the pkg-config utility via the #cgo pkg-config: directive.

Then you define a Go struct that will hold a pointer to the sb_stemmer C struct:

nongo/stem/stem.go
```
// Stemmer stems words for a specific language.
type Stemmer struct {
    st *C.struct_sb_stemmer
}
```

The C struct name is sb_stemmer, but in Go we reference it as C.struct_sb_stemmer.

Next, you write NewStemmer to create a new Stemmer and initialize the underlying C struct:

```
nongo/stem/stem.go
// NewStemmer creates a new stemmer for a language.
func NewStemmer(lang string) (*Stemmer, error) {
    cLang := C.CString(lang) // Go -> C string
    st := C.sb_stemmer_new(cLang, nil)
    C.free(unsafe.Pointer(cLang))

    if st == nil {
        return nil, fmt.Errorf("can't create stemmer for %q", lang)
    }

    return &Stemmer{st}, nil
}
```

In line 3, you convert the Go string to a C string. This allocates memory for the new C string. In line 5, you free this allocated memory.

To free the memory allocated by C in NewStemmer, you provide a Close method:

```
nongo/stem/stem.go
// Close closes the stemmer, freeing allocated memory.
func (s *Stemmer) Close() {
    if s.st != nil {
        C.sb_stemmer_delete(s.st)
        s.st = nil
    }
}
```

Now you can write the Stem method, which gets a string and returns a string:

```
nongo/stem/stem.go
// Stem will stem a word.
// In case of error will return the empty string
func (s *Stemmer) Stem(word string) string {
```

You start by converting the Go string to the data type that's accepted by the C sb_stemmer_stem function and then call this function:

```
nongo/stem/stem.go
cWord := C.CBytes([]byte(word))
size := C.int(len(word))
sym := C.sb_stemmer_stem(s.st, (*C.uchar)(cWord), size)
if sym == nil {
    return ""
}
```

And at the end, you convert the value returned from C into a Go string:

```
nongo/stem/stem.go
// Convert to Go string
i := C.sb_stemmer_length(s.st)
```

```
data := C.GoBytes(unsafe.Pointer(sym), i)
```

```
// No need to free data, managed by C stemmer
return string(data)
```

Finally, you write a small test:

```
nongo/stem/stem.go
s, err := NewStemmer("en")
if err != nil {
    log.Fatalf("error: %s", err)
}
defer s.Close()

for _, w := range []string{"works", "working", "worked"} {
    stem := s.Stem(w)
    fmt.Printf("%-8s → %s\n", w, stem)
}
```

Running this code gives you this output:

```
works    → work
working  → work
worked   → work
```

Discussion

Calling C with basic types, such as numbers and bytes, is pretty easy. Things become more complex when types are more complex.

In this case, we're dealing with strings and need to convert them back and forth and also be sure to manually free some memory.

On the bright side, we now have a fully functioning, battle-tested stemmer in less than one hundred lines of code.

Final Thoughts

At some point or another, you'll use cgo to interact with existing code written in C (or C++). If you can avoid using cgo, by all means do so. cgo carries a lot of operational complexity—finding header files and libraries, building for specific operating systems, and more.

One of the main issues when working with C is memory management. Pay special attention to *who* is allocating memory and when it should be freed. When in doubt, copy the memory you need.

And finally, you need to know C, at least at the basic level. The good news is that C is a simple language and has a lot in common with Go. The main issue

I face when writing Go and C together is to remember when to write i int and when to write int i. Lucky for me, the compiler tells me when I'm wrong (which is too often).

os/exec is a safer and easier option to reuse existing code. But it requires that there's an executable capable of doing what you need on the machine running your code—this might not always be the case.

No matter which path you take, cgo or os/exec, make sure it's worth the risk and operational complexity.

Next, we'll see how you can test your code.

## CHAPTER 13

Testing Your Code

Testing is important. It's the safety net that guards us against our own inability to reason about complex systems.

Go comes with a built-in test suite called testing. Like most of Go, it's simple and gets the job done.

In the following recipes, we're going to explore how to use the testing package effectively.

Recipe 65

Conditionally Running Continuous Integration Tests

Task

Your project is getting good test coverage. Developers are required to make sure the tests pass before committing code. But now the average test suite runtime is about twenty minutes. Waiting that long for the tests to finish starts to impact productivity.

After a heated discussion, Ben, the team lead, decides to split the tests into two groups. The first group will run on a developer machine and should not take more than five minutes. The second group will run only in the continuous integration (CI) system and can run for a longer time.

Continuous Integration

A continuous integration (CI) system is one that automatically runs whenever someone commits code to a central repository.

The term *continuous integration* was coined by Martin Fowler.[1]

Of course, this task falls on you …

Solution

You look at your CI system and see that it automatically sets an environment variable called CI. You set a global isCi flag at when the tests start:

testing/ci/report_test.go
```go
var (
    inCi = os.Getenv("CI") != ""
)
```

And then you can skip CI tests if isCi is false:

testing/ci/report_test.go
```go
func TestMonthlyReport(t *testing.T) {
    if !inCi {
        t.Skip("not in CI system")
    }

    t.Log("running in CI")
    // TODO: Rest of long running test ...
}
```

Running the tests on a developer machine shows it skips TestMonthlyReport:

```
$ go test -v
=== RUN    TestMonthlyReport
    report_test.go:18: not in CI system
--- SKIP: TestMonthlyReport (0.00s)
PASS
ok      github.com/353solutions/go-cookbook/ci   0.001s
```

When you want to run this test, you can emulate a CI environment by setting the CI environment variable:

```
$ CI=true go test -v
=== RUN    TestMonthlyReport
    report_test.go:21: running in CI
--- PASS: TestMonthlyReport (0.00s)
PASS
ok      github.com/353solutions/go-cookbook/ci   0.001s
```

---

1.   https://www.martinfowler.com/articles/continuousIntegration.html

Discussion

testint/T.Skip will stop the current test execution and report the test as skipped. Any code after t.Skip() will not be executed.

Using environment variables allows developers to quickly run tests that are meant to run only in CI. You can combine setting the CI environment variable with the -run flag for go test to run only a single CI test:

```
$ CI=true go test -run TestMonthlyReport -v
=== RUN    TestMonthlyReport
    report_test.go:21: running in CI
--- PASS: TestMonthlyReport (0.00s)
PASS
ok      github.com/353solutions/go-cookbook/ci  0.001s
```

You'll find other reasons for writing tests that run only in CI. Sometimes there are tests that require a complicated setup that's not possible on a developer machine. In other cases, you might need special hardware that not every developer has.

No matter what the case is, try to keep your developers happy. If your developers need to work hard to run the tests, they'll start cutting corners.

I highly recommend you use a CI system—at one point or another it will save you from the dreadful "works on my machine" bug. You don't have to host a CI system (such as Jenkins) yourself. Many services offer CI—GitHub Actions, CircleCI, and GitLab CI/CD, just to name a few. In these systems, all you need to do is to provide a configuration file on how to run the tests, and the CI system will take care of the rest. Some of them even report the CI status on a pull request or provide markdown badges for your project's REAMDE.md file.

Recipe 66

Reading Test Cases from a File

Task

You're working in a company that develops an automated storehouse.

Your job is to calculate how many boxes are needed to pack a specific cart full of items.

Bin Packing

In the general form, this problem is known as the "Bin packing problem" and is proven to be NP-hard. We won't go down the rabbit hole of what NP-hard is—if you're curious, you can start at Wikipedia.[2] I hope to see you back soon.

After some discussions, you start by writing a simple greedy algorithm that considers only the weight of the items:

testing/packer/packer.go

```go
// Item is an package item.
type Item struct {
    Name    string
    Weight float64
}

// Pack returns items split to boxes.
// It considers item weight only and uses a greedy algorithm.
func Pack(boxCap float64, cart []Item) ([][]Item, error) {
    var boxes [][]Item
    weight := 0.0
    var box []Item
    for _, item := range cart {
        if item.Weight > boxCap {
            const format = "item %#v too heavy for %f"
            return nil, fmt.Errorf(format, item, boxCap)
        }

        if weight+item.Weight > boxCap { // need a new box
            boxes = append(boxes, box)
            box = []Item{}
            weight = 0.0
        }

        box = append(box, item)
        weight += item.Weight
    }
    if len(box) > 0 { // add sentinel
        boxes = append(boxes, box)
    }

    return boxes, nil
}
```

2. en.wikipedia.org/wiki/NP-hardness

Eva, the QA lead, opens the following issue:

> We want to test the Pack function. However, we'd like to add test cases as we go along, and we don't want to write Go code. Please find a way for us to write test cases in plain text. Formats such as JSON or YAML are OK as well.

Solution

You agree with the QA team on using YAML for specifying tests.

Here's an example input file:

testing/packer/packer_cases.yml
```yaml
- name: simple
  err: false
  box_capacity: 6
  weights:
    - 2.3
    - 3.7
    - 5
  num_boxes: 2
- name: over
  err: true
  box_capacity: 10
  weights:
    - 1.2
    - 37
    - 9.5
```

Once the team agrees on the input format, you can start writing the code.

You start by writing a TestCase struct:

testing/packer/packer_test.go
```go
type TestCase struct {
    Name      string    `yaml:"name"`
    BoxCap    float64   `yaml:"box_capacity"`
    N         int       `yaml:"num_boxes"`
    Weights   []float64 `yaml:"weights"`
    ShouldErr bool      `yaml:"err"`
}
```

Then you write code to load test cases from a YAML file:

testing/packer/packer_test.go
```go
func loadCases(t *testing.T, path string) []TestCase {
    file, err := os.Open(path)
    if err != nil {
        t.Fatal(err)
    }
```

```
    defer file.Close()
    var tcs []TestCase
    if err := yaml.NewDecoder(file).Decode(&tcs); err != nil {
        t.Fatal(err)
    }
    return tcs
}
```

Before you can write the test, you need to convert the slice of weights from the input file to a slice of Item:

testing/packer/packer_test.go
```
func weightsToItems(ws []float64) []Item {
    items := make([]Item, 0, len(ws))
    for i, w := range ws {
        item := Item{
            Name:   fmt.Sprintf("item %d", i+1),
            Weight: w,
        }
        items = append(items, item)
    }
    return items
}
```

Now that the infrastructure is ready, you can write the test code:

testing/packer/packer_test.go
```
Line 1  func TestPack(t *testing.T) {
   -        testCases := loadCases(t, "packer_cases.yml")
   -        for _, tc := range testCases {
   -            items := weightsToItems(tc.Weights)
   5            t.Run(tc.Name, func(t *testing.T) {
   -                boxes, err := Pack(tc.BoxCap, items)
   -                if err == nil && tc.ShouldErr {
   -                    t.Fatal("expected error, got nil")
   -                }
  10                if err != nil && !tc.ShouldErr {
   -                    t.Fatalf("unexpected error: %s", err)
   -                }
   -
   -                if n := len(boxes); n != tc.N {
  15                    t.Fatalf("expected %d boxes, got %d", tc.N, n)
   -                }
   -            })
   -        }
   -  }
```

You're happy to see that the test passes:

```
$ go test -v
=== RUN    TestPack
=== RUN    TestPack/simple
=== RUN    TestPack/over
--- PASS: TestPack (0.00s)
    --- PASS: TestPack/simple (0.00s)
    --- PASS: TestPack/over (0.00s)
PASS
ok      github.com/353solutions/go-cookbook/packer      0.002s
```

Discussion

loadCases does not follow the idiomatic Go way of returning an error value. It accepts a *testing.T argument and uses its Fatal method on error. Calling t.Fatal will halt the current test. It's common to test helper functions in this manner. Instead of returning errors, the testing code becomes shorter and clearer.

In line 5, we start a subtest. Using subtests greatly helps to detect the input that caused an error. We use the name given in the input YAML as the name of the tests; you can see it in the preceding test output.

Using a format that lets non-coders specify test cases will reduce the amount of work for developers. Most non-coders can write YAML without much trouble, and since it's an established format, it already has a parser you can use.

Recipe 67

Fuzzing Bugs Away

Task

The current implementation of your service is using a map to store users. The service becomes very popular, and this map becomes too big to fit in memory.

After some research and discussions, you decide to use a Bloom filter[3] to save memory.

A Bloom filter requires a long sequence of bits—more than the 64 an integer can hold. You start writing a BitArray data type, which uses a []byte. You need

---

3. https://redis.com/blog/bloom-filter/

to know how many bytes, each holding 8 bits, are required to hold n bits. You write the following function:

```
testing/bloom/bloom.go
// NumBytes returns the number of bytes that can hold n bits.
func NumBytes(nBits int) int {
    return (nBits + 7) / 8
}
```

Now you'd like to test NumBytes.

Solution

You decide to use the testing package and write a fuzz test function that uses random values:

```
testing/bloom/bloom_test.go
Line 1  func FuzzNumBytes(f *testing.F) {
    -       f.Add(0)
    -
    -       fn := func(t *testing.T, n int) {
    5           // Ignore negative numbers
    -           if n < 0 {
    -               return
    -           }
    -           nBytes := NumBytes(n)
   10           ok := (nBytes*8 >= n) && ((nBytes-1)*8 <= n)
    -           if !ok {
    -               t.Fatal(nBytes)
    -           }
    -       }
   15       f.Fuzz(fn)
    -   }
```

Discussion

You need to supply the fuzzer a function that accepts a *testing.T and variable number of parameters. You define the function, called fn, in line 4. fn will call NumBytes with a random number generated by testing/quick and will call t.Fail if NumBytes returns incorrect output. Since n can be any number, you decide to ignore negative values.

In line 2, you call f.Fuzz to add known examples you want to check.

In line 15, you call f.Fuzz. It will analyze the function signature, and for each parameter it will generate a random value and pass these values to your test function (fn).

The hard part is to figure out a heuristic that reveals if the tested function succeeded or failed, given a random input.

Our heuristic is in line 10. We take the output of NumBytes, called nBytes, and check that it's just the right number of bytes to hold n bits.

If the heuristic holds, it means you've found the right number of bytes—not too many and not too few.

To run the fuzz test, you execute the code:

```
$ go test -run NONE -fuzz . -fuzztime 10s
fuzz: elapsed: 0s, gathering baseline coverage: 0/2 completed
fuzz: elapsed: 0s, gathering baseline coverage: 2/2 completed, \
    now fuzzing with 12 workers
fuzz: elapsed: 3s, execs: 539516 (179825/sec), new interesting: 0 (total: 2)
fuzz: elapsed: 6s, execs: 1095318 (185253/sec), new interesting: 0 (total: 2)
fuzz: elapsed: 9s, execs: 1661641 (188757/sec), new interesting: 0 (total: 2)
fuzz: elapsed: 10s, execs: 1848027 (170329/sec), new interesting: 0 (total: 2)
PASS
```

The fuzz function will continue to run until it finds a failing example. You use -fuzztime 10s to limit the fuzz execution. If the fuzz function finds a failing example, it will record it under testdata/fuzz and will try the example next time you run the fuzzer.

You didn't think about negative numbers!

Finding a good heuristic might be difficult at times, but with some creative thinking you can find one that is good enough to uncover some bugs.

The built-in fuzzer supports generating random values only for the following types:

- string, []byte
- int, int8, int16, int32/rune, int64
- uint, uint8, uint16, uint32, uint64
- float32, float64
- bool

If you have more-complex data types, you'll need to be creative or use the older (but still functional) testing/quick package.

Try to add some kind of fuzzing in your tests—you're bound to find a lot of interesting bugs. Many libraries, even some in the Go standard library, report finding bugs using fuzzing.

Mocking HTTP Client Calls

Task

Your server has a REST API, and you just got the following issue:

> We'd like to write a client for the REST API. The client will expose methods and hide the implementation details from users. Hiding the REST API details from the user will allow us to change the REST API structure in the future or even switch to another RPC framework, such as gRPC, without forcing clients to change their code.

You work on the issue and come up with the following code:

```
testing/mock/httpc.go
// APIClient is an API client.
type APIClient struct {
    baseURL string
    c       *http.Client
}

// NewAPIClient returns a new APIClient.
func NewAPIClient(baseURL string) *APIClient {
    return &APIClient{baseURL, &http.Client{}}
}
```

Now, you'd like to test the Users method:

```
testing/mock/httpc.go
// Users returns the list of users.
func (c *APIClient) Users() ([]string, error) {
    url := fmt.Sprintf("%s/users", c.baseURL)
    resp, err := c.c.Get(url)
    if err != nil {
        return nil, err
    }
    defer resp.Body.Close()

    var users []string
    if err := json.NewDecoder(resp.Body).Decode(&users); err != nil {
        return nil, err
    }

    return users, nil
}
```

But you want to test it without running the server, which has a complicated setup and is a resource hog.

Solution

You define a MockTransport struct that implements the http.RoundTripper interface:

testing/mock/httpc_test.go
```
Line 1   type MockTransport struct {
             body []byte
             err  error
         }

    5
         // RoundTrip implements http.RoundTripper
         func (t *MockTransport) RoundTrip(r *http.Request) (*http.Response, error) {
             if t.err != nil {
                 return nil, t.err
   10        }

             w := httptest.NewRecorder()
             if t.body != nil {
                 w.Write(t.body)
   15        }
             return w.Result(), nil
         }
```

Now you can replace the APIClient internal HTTP client Transport with the mock transport. You start by writing a test for the happy path:

testing/mock/httpc_test.go
```
func TestUsersOK(t *testing.T) {
    users := []string{"clark", "diana", "bruce"}
    data, err := json.Marshal(users)
    require.NoError(t, err, "encode JSON")

    c := NewAPIClient("http://localhost:8080")
    c.c.Transport = &MockTransport{data, nil}
    reply, err := c.Users()
    require.NoError(t, err, "API call")
    require.Equal(t, users, reply, "users")
}
```

Then you emulate a connection error:

testing/mock/httpc_test.go
```
func TestUsersConnectionError(t *testing.T) {
    c := NewAPIClient("http://localhost:8080")
    c.c.Transport = &MockTransport{nil, fmt.Errorf("network error")}
    _, err := c.Users()
    require.Error(t, err)
}
```

And finally, you emulate errors in transport by sending back bad JSON:

```
testing/mock/httpc_test.go
func TestUsersBadJSON(t *testing.T) {
    c := NewAPIClient("http://localhost:8080")
    c.c.Transport = &MockTransport{[]byte(`["clark","diana","bruce"`), nil}
    _, err := c.Users()
    require.Error(t, err)
}
```

Discussion

The Go team thought about testability when designing Go's data structures. In most places when you need to customize or mock behavior, you'll find interfaces.

The net/http.Client has a RoundTripper field that it uses for doing the actual call. We're creating our own mock RoundTripper that can emulate networking errors, bad data, and many other scenarios that are close to impossible to create with real servers.

The http.Response structure has many fields. It's easier to use the ResponseRecoder from the http/httptest package, like we do in line 12, than to populate all the required fields manually.

Some teams don't like it when tests make HTTP calls. The reason is the network is not reliable 100% of the time, so some tests fail because of these network errors. The network can get congested and slow down, which makes having timeouts for tests a tricky thing as well.

You need to keep in mind that every time you use a mock, you're cheating. In the above three tests, we didn't call the real server. For example, if someone changes the /users API to be under /api/users, our tests will pass but the code running against the server will fail.

If you need more mocking capabilities, such as checking if functions were called, checking return arguments, and more, have a look at the github.com/stretchr/testify/mock package.

Recipe 69

Writing Global Setup/Teardown Functions

Task

You're working on improving your test suite. Looking at the tests, you see many of them create a temporary configuration in YAML format. For all the tests, the configuration file is the same.

Helen, with whom you share an office, suggests writing the configuration file when the tests start. You think it's a good idea and convince your boss that this is your next task. At the end of the tests, you'd like to delete this file.

Solution

You start by writing the setup code for the tests, which generates a configuration file:

```
testing/testmain/main_test.go
const (
    envConfigKey = "APP_CONFIG_FILE"
)

func setupTests() error {
    file, err := os.CreateTemp("", "*.yml")
    if err != nil {
        return err
    }
    defer file.Close()

    cfg := map[string]any{
        "verbose": true,
        "dsn":     "postgres://localhost:5432",
    }
    if err := yaml.NewEncoder(file).Encode(cfg); err != nil {
        return err
    }

    os.Setenv(envConfigKey, file.Name())
    log.Printf("config file: %q", file.Name())
    return nil
}
```

You also write the teardown code that will remove the configuration file:

```
testing/testmain/main_test.go
func teardownTests() {
    fileName := os.Getenv(envConfigKey)
    if err := os.Remove(fileName); err != nil {
        log.Printf("warning: can't delete %q - %s", fileName, err)
    }
}
```

Then you write a runTests function:

```
testing/testmain/main_test.go
func runTests(m *testing.M) int {
    if err := setupTests(); err != nil {
        log.Printf("error: can't setup tests - %s", err)
        return 1
    }
    defer teardownTests()
    return m.Run()
}
```

And finally, you write TestMain:

```
testing/testmain/main_test.go
func TestMain(m *testing.M) {
    code := runTests(m)
    os.Exit(code)
}
```

Discussion

TestMain is a special function. The testing module says:

> To support these and other cases, if a test file contains a function:
>
> ```
> func TestMain(m *testing.M)
> ```
>
> then the generated test will call TestMain(m) instead of running the tests directly.

The purpose of TestMain is to enable writing global setup and teardown functions (sometimes called *fixtures*). The reason we write runTests is that os.Exit will exit the program without invoking deferred functions. runTests enables us to write idiomatic defer for teardown code. We return the value from m.Run to TestMain, which calls os.Exit *after* the deferred teardownTests is called.

It's important to exit your program (including tests) in a non-zero exit code when there's an error—this signals the caller that there was a failure.

In some cases, you might want to keep some test resources around so you can debug them. Try changing the code so it'll delete the configuration file only if m.Run() returns 0.

Running Services in Testing

Task

Your boss opens the following issue:

> We're using too many mocks and testing/httptest in our tests, and it feels like cheating. I'd like you to write a test that runs the actual server and then run end-to-end tests on it.

You think about it in your next jogging session and decide to use os/exec to run the server.

Solution

You start by writing code that will build the server executable:

testing/srv_test/httpd_test.go
```
func buildServer(t *testing.T) string {
    fileName := path.Join(t.TempDir(), "httpd")
    cmd := exec.Command("go", "build", "-o", fileName, "httpd.go")
    if err := cmd.Run(); err != nil {
        t.Fatal(err)
    }

    return fileName
}
```

To run the server, you need to find a free port on the local machine:

testing/srv_test/httpd_test.go
```
func freePort(t *testing.T) int {
    conn, err := net.Listen("tcp", "")
    if err != nil {
        t.Fatal(err)
    }

    conn.Close()
    return conn.Addr().(*net.TCPAddr).Port
}
```

The server takes some time to load, so you write a function that will wait for the server to load and fail if it doesn't answer after a timeout:

testing/srv_test/httpd_test.go
```go
func waitForServer(t *testing.T, addr string) {
    start := time.Now()
    timeout := 10 * time.Second
    var err error
    var conn net.Conn
    for time.Since(start) < timeout {
        conn, err = net.Dial("tcp", addr)
        if err == nil {
            conn.Close()
            return
        }
        time.Sleep(10 * time.Millisecond)
    }

    t.Fatalf("server not ready after %s (%s)", timeout, err)
}
```

Now you can write the code that starts the server on a random port and returns the port number.

testing/srv_test/httpd_test.go
```go
func runServer(t *testing.T) int {
    exe := buildServer(t)
    t.Logf("server exe: %q", exe)
    port := freePort(t)
    t.Logf("server port: %d", port)

    env := os.Environ()
    env = append(env, fmt.Sprintf("HTTPD_ADDR=:%d", port))
    cmd := exec.Command(exe)
    cmd.Env = env
    err := cmd.Start()
    if err != nil {
        t.Fatal(err)
    }

    addr := fmt.Sprintf("localhost:%d", port)
    waitForServer(t, addr)
    t.Cleanup(func() {
        if err := cmd.Process.Kill(); err != nil {
            t.Logf("warning: can't kill server (pid=%d)", cmd.Process.Pid)
        }
    })

    return port
}
```

Once runServer is ready, you can use it in a test:

testing/srv_test/httpd_test.go
```go
func TestHealth(t *testing.T) {
    port := runServer(t)

    url := fmt.Sprintf("http://localhost:%d/health", port)
    resp, err := http.Get(url)
    if err != nil {
        t.Fatal(err)
    }

    if resp.StatusCode != http.StatusOK {
        t.Fatalf("bad return code: %d", resp.StatusCode)
    }
}
```

Discussion

The testing utility functions, such as buildServer, don't return an error. They accept a *testing.T and call Fatal on error. This coding style differs from the regular Go style where you return errors from functions, but it makes the testing code shorter and clearer.

You need to terminate the server process after the test is done, but you create it in runServer. This is where t.Cleanup comes in handy—it'll call a function only when the test is done.

Your HTTP server needs to support a configurable port to listen on via environment variables. In line 10, you set the environment for the process, using the Cmd.Env field.

You might wonder why you should build the server and run it instead of using go run. The reason is that go run creates a subprocess, so the Kill in line 19 will kill the go process but not the underlying server process.

It might seem like a lot of code to start a test, but these end-to-end tests are important—you're testing a scenario closer to production.

Recipe 71

Writing a Linter

Task

After some nasty bugs in production, the Go guild in your company is discussing how you can catch errors earlier in the development process. One of the issues is how you can disallow the use of forbidden packages.

You write the following in the guild chat:

> You: What about writing a linter that will check for disallowed packages?
>
> Mariana: Go for it!

Since Mariana is your boss, you go for it.

Solution

You start by importing several packages from golang.org/x/tools/go/analysis:

testing/lint/forbidden.go
```
import (
    "fmt"
    "go/ast"
    "os"
    "strings"

    "golang.org/x/tools/go/analysis"
    "golang.org/x/tools/go/analysis/passes/inspect"
    "golang.org/x/tools/go/analysis/singlechecker"
    "golang.org/x/tools/go/ast/inspector"
)
```

Then you list the forbidden packages:

testing/lint/forbidden.go
```
forbidden = []string{
    "syscall",
    // TODO: More packages to forbid
}
```

And you write a function to check if a package (import path) is forbidden:

testing/lint/forbidden.go

```go
func isForbidden(path string) bool {
    for _, prefix := range forbidden {
        if strings.HasPrefix(path, prefix) {
            return true
        }
    }
    return false
}
```

Then you define an Analyzer:

testing/lint/forbidden.go

```go
Analyzer = &analysis.Analyzer{
    Name:     "forbidden",
    Doc:      "Check for usage of forbidden packages",
    Requires: []*analysis.Analyzer{inspect.Analyzer},
    Run:      run,
}
```

At last, you write the run function that will analyze the code:

testing/lint/forbidden.go

```go
func run(pass *analysis.Pass) (any, error) {
    filter := []ast.Node{
        (*ast.ImportSpec)(nil),
    }

    inspect := pass.ResultOf[inspect.Analyzer].(*inspector.Inspector)
    inspect.Preorder(filter, func(node ast.Node) {
        imp, ok := node.(*ast.ImportSpec)
        if !ok {
            pos := pass.Fset.Position(node.Pos())
            fname, lnum := pos.Filename, pos.Line
            const warnFmt = "%s:%d: warning: not an import\n"
            fmt.Fprintf(os.Stderr, warnFmt, fname, lnum)
            return
        }

        // `"syscall"` -> `syscall`
        path := strings.Trim(imp.Path.Value, `"`)
        if !isForbidden(path) {
            return
        }
        pass.Reportf(imp.Pos(), "importing forbidden package %q", path)
    })

    return nil, nil
}
```

You first run a pass of inspect.Analyzer and then use its output to run a preorder walk only on nodes of type ast.ImportSpec. When you find a forbidden package, you use Reportf to report the offending line.

Finally, you write a show main, using the singlechecker.Main:

testing/lint/forbidden.go
```
func main() {
    singlechecker.Main(Analyzer)
}
```

To test the package, you create a file with some errors and annotate the offending lines with a comment indicating the expected linter output for this line:

testing/lint/testdata/app.go
```
package main

import (
    "fmt"
    "syscall" // want `importing forbidden package "syscall"`
)

func main() {
    fmt.Println(syscall.AF_ALG)
}
```

Once you have an example, you write a show test, using analysistest.TestData:

testing/lint/forbidden_test.go
```
package main

import (
    "testing"

    "golang.org/x/tools/go/analysis/analysistest"
)

func TestAnalyzer(t *testing.T) {
    analysistest.Run(t, analysistest.TestData(), Analyzer)
}
```

Discussion

The cost of fixing an error goes up the further away from the point you introduced it. Think how much it'll cost you to find a syntax error versus how much it'll cost you to fix a bug in the production server. Writing tools like our linter will detect bugs closer to where they were introduced and will save you money in the long run.

From the beginning, Go was designed to be "tool friendly."

The golang.org/x/tools/go/analysis package was written to help with writing tools that analyze code.

Your linter code is about fifty-five lines of code!

The last step is to add the linter as part of your test suite. Once the linter runs as part of the test suite, developers won't forget to run it. In my projects, we run linters, such as https://staticcheck.io, *before* we run the tests. If the linter fails, we don't bother to run the tests—we mark them as failed right there.

Running linters and then tests makes running the tests more than one command. To make sure people won't mess up, use an automation tool, such as make, or a script that will run all the steps required for the tests. Make sure your CI system runs all the steps, as well, probably by running make or your custom script.

Final Thoughts

You can never write enough tests! If you look at the SQLite documentation,[4] you'll see they have 640 lines of testing code for every source line. And even so, SQLite has bugs!

Testing is a balance between "pain versus gain." The pain is writing tests. It takes development effort to write tests, and once you have a big enough test suite, making big changes takes longer. The gain is the damage you'll prevent. If you write an internal system for picking where to go to lunch at work, bugs don't hurt that much. If you write code that navigates airplanes, bugs can cost lives.

Do your own pain-versus-gain balance and make an informed decision on how much to invest in testing.

No matter how rigorous the development and testing, you *will* have bugs in production. NASA[5] has a very thorough development process, but they still manage to ship bugs to Mars. On the flip side, NASA can also fix bugs on Mars. I find this mind-boggling!

Next, we'll have a look at what happens after you test your code—it's time to build your code.

---

4. https://www.sqlite.org/testing.html
5. https://www.fastcompany.com/28121/they-write-right-stuff

## CHAPTER 14

Building Applications

Building your code seems simple—run go build, and you're done!

In some cases, you'll need more flexibility in your builds. For example, you might want to build for a different platform than the one you're developing on or maybe add assets to your binary.

The go build command has many features that can accommodate most of your needs. In this chapter, we're going to explore some of the more useful build commands and tricks. We'll look into code generation, cross compilation, injecting version and assets into your binary, and more.

Recipe 72

Embedding Assets in Your Binary

Task

Your application is providing data by querying a database. The BI (business intelligence) team writes the SQL queries to the database.

In the morning stand-up, Agnes shares an incident from last night:

> One of the database queries had an error that caused the daily user handlers to fail. The root cause was a cut-and-paste error from the BI SQL file into the Go file. We did a code review but missed a dash in a SQL comment.

The team agrees they need to write tests to cover SQL changes, but it'll take time to create a test database and write the tests. In the meantime, you suggest to keep SQL in .sql files and not verbatim in the Go code. This will allow using common SQL tools on the files, and you'll also get syntax highlighting.

Your team lead agrees and asks you to make the change.

Solution

You move each query to its own .sql file, like this, for example:

building/embed/user.sql
```sql
SELECT id, name, email
FROM users
WHERE id = @id
;
```

Next, in your code you underscore import the embed package:

building/embed/users.go
```go
import (
    "database/sql"
    _ "embed"
)
```

Then you define a userSQL variable that will be populated by the embed package:

building/embed/users.go
```go
//
//go:embed user.sql
var userSQL string
```

Finally, you can use userSQL in your code:

building/embed/users.go
```go
// User is a user in the system.
type User struct {
    ID    string // UUID
    Name  string
    Email string
}

// UserByID returns user by ID
func UserByID(db *sql.DB, id string) (User, error) {
    row := db.QueryRow(userSQL, sql.Named("id", id))
    var u User
    err := row.Scan(&u.ID, &u.Name, &u.Email)
    return u, err
}
```

Discussion

The embed package was added in Go 1.16. It allows you to embed assets (files) in your Go executable. Using embed gives you ease of development with multiple files and ease of deployment with a single executable.

You need to have a //go:embed <filename> directive in the line before the variable that you want populated. If the file is not found, the build will fail.

You can also embed directories; the variable after the //go:embed directive should be an embed.FS. embed.FS is an abstract file system, which allows you to open files as if they are on the local file system. The built-in net/http.FileServer server can serve files directly from an embed.FS variable. This way, you can embed all of your front-end assets, such as Javascript, CSS files, and images from a directory into a single executable.

Recipe 73

Injecting Version to Your Executable

Task

You are the owner of an agent that your company ships to customers. Joice, one of the support engineers, opens the following issue one cool afternoon:

> The agent has several versions now. When we get an error message from a customer, it will be helpful to know what the version is of the agent they are running. In some cases, the solution to their problem is a simple upgrade. Can you please add a -version flag?

You think, how did we miss that? and start working on the issue.

Solution

You start by defining a version variable:

building/agent/agent.go
```
var (
    version = "<unknown>"
)
```

Then you add a command-line flag to show the agent version and exit:

building/agent/agent.go

```
var showVersion bool
flag.BoolVar(&showVersion, "version", false, "show version and exit")
flag.Parse()

if showVersion {
    fmt.Printf("agent version %s\n", version)
}
```

Now you turn to building. You write a Go utility to run the build. First is a small function to run a command and return its output:

building/agent/_scripts/build.go

```
func run(args ...string) (string, error) {
    cmd := exec.Command(args[0], args[1:]...)
    out, err := cmd.CombinedOutput()
    if err != nil {
        return "", err
    }
    return strings.TrimSpace(string(out)), nil
}
```

Once run is in place, you can start building. You start by trying to get the current git tag:

building/agent/_scripts/build.go

```
version, err := run("git", "tag", "--points-at", "HEAD")
if err != nil {
    log.Fatalf("error: %s", err)
}
```

If you can't find a git tag, you use the current git commit as a version:

building/agent/_scripts/build.go

```
if version == "" {
    var err error
    version, err = run("git", "rev-parse", "--short", "HEAD")
    if err != nil {
        log.Fatalf("error: %s", err)
    }
}
```

Finally, you call go build and pass ldflags to set the version value in the generated binary:

building/agent/_scripts/build.go

```
log.Printf("building version %s\n", version)
ldflags := fmt.Sprintf("-ldflags=-X main.version=%s", version)
_, err = run("go", "build", ldflags, "-o", "agent")
```

```
if err != nil {
    log.Fatalf("error: %s", err)
}
```

Discussion

You use -ldflags flags, which is described here:

```
> -ldflags '[pattern=]arg list'
>         arguments to pass on each go tool link invocation.
```

To view the options of the link tool, run go tool link -help, and you will see the following:

```
> -X definition
>         add string value definition of the form importpath.name=value
```

This help fragment means you can set the value of a variable at compile time.

The variable you're changing doesn't have to start with an uppercase letter (exported).

You can add a version to your code in many ways:

- Use tools such as sed or awk to change a version string in the code
- Override a version.go file with the current version
- Use ldflags

The latter is simpler, doesn't require external tools (such as sed), and doesn't change the sources.

By using a build.go utility, you stay with Go. You could have written the same tool in Bash or Python, probably in less lines of code, but you would have introduced a new language. Developers need to learn about these new languages, and you need to make sure these tools are available on the build machine. build.go comes to about thirty-five lines of code—the trade-off between staying with Go and shorter script is well worth it.

build.go is in a folder called _scripts; the go build command ignores directories that start with underscore (_). For extra caution, you also add a //go:build ignore directive to build.go, as this will make sure go build ignores it. And if you have more than one tool at _scripts, it will prevent linters from marking a duplicate main as an error.

Semantic Versioning

The Go module system works best if you use semantic versioning. A version should be in the format v1.2.3, where 3 is the patch level and should be bug fixes only, 2 is a minor version and should be used for added features, and 1 is the major version, where changes can be backward incompatible. Think long and hard before changing major versions.

To learn more about semantic versioning, visit https://semver.org/. You should also probably visit the "Versions" section in the "go mod" documentation at https://go.dev/ref/mod.

Recipe 74

Ensuring Static Builds

Task

Your continuous integration (CI) system is building the agent using Docker. The operations team are working on CI changes, and they open a new issue for you to puzzle on:

> We're packing your application in a docker container. When we try to run the agent inside the container, we see something odd:

```
$ ./agent
/bin/sh: ./agent: not found
```

> But the file is there:

```
$ ls agent
agent
```

> Any ideas how to fix this?

You start to investigate.

Solution

Talking to the operations team, you find out they use Alpine Docker. You run the operations to build the container:

```
$ docker run --rm -it cookbook/agent /bin/sh
/ #
```

Then you investigate further, using the file utility (which you need to install):

```
$ file agent
agent: ELF 64-bit LSB executable, x86-64, version 1 (SYSV), \
    dynamically linked, interpreter /lib64/ld-linux-x86-64.so.2, \
    Go BuildID=LE58LuxUxKGFaRWCtMu2/pUGr5jXM4dPOPD1dUsJF/... \
    with debug_info, not stripped
```

Two things capture your attention: dynamically linked and interpreter /lib64/ld-linux-x86-64.so.2. dynamically linked means this executable depends on shared libraries. But the go build command should produce static executables that do not depend on external shared libraries.

go build will produce a dynamically linked executable if you're using cgo, but this isn't the case here.

interpreter /lib64/ld-linux-x86-64.so.2 is what is used to run the executable, so you do a quick check:

```
$ ls /lib64/ld-linux-x86-64.so.2
ls: /lib64/ld-linux-x86-64.so.2: No such file or directory
```

You use the ldd utility to verify that your assumptions are right:

```
$ ldd agent
        /lib64/ld-linux-x86-64.so.2 (0x7fbc120e7000)
        libc.so.6 => /lib64/ld-linux-x86-64.so.2 (0x7fbc120e7000)
```

You then look at the imports in agent.go:

building/agent/agent.go
```
import (
    "context"
    "flag"
    "fmt"
    "net/http"
    "time"
)
```

Nothing seems out of place, but then you remember reading something about net/http and cgo. You head over to the net package documentation[1] and reach the "Name Resolution" section, where it says:

> On Unix systems, the resolver has two options for resolving names. It can use a pure Go resolver that sends DNS requests directly to the servers listed in /etc/resolv.conf, or it can use a cgo-based resolver that calls C-library routines such as getaddrinfo and getnameinfo.

---

1. https://golang.org/pkg/net/

> By default the pure Go resolver is used, because a blocked DNS request consumes only a goroutine, while a blocked C call consumes an operating system thread. *When cgo is available, the cgo-based resolver is used instead under a variety of conditions ...*

The preceding section explains why you got a dynamically linked executable, but why isn't it running on your machine?

You're building in a debian docker with the same architecture (amd64) as your machine.

Then you remember operations are using Alpine Docker to package the agent. An Alpine Docker image is small, in part by using musl, which is a replacement for libc.

You have two options—either use another Docker image or force static builds. You decide to go with the second option.

You head over to the cgo documentation[2] and find out:

> You can control this by setting the CGO_ENABLED environment variable when running the go tool: set it to 1 to enable the use of cgo and to 0 to disable it.

After reading the preceding documentation, you decide to set CGO_ENABLED=0 in the environment and check.

First, you try it locally:

```
$ CGO_ENABLED=0 go build -o agent agent.go
$ ldd agent
    not a dynamic executable
```

Then you fix your Dockerfile by adding the following line before the go build command:

```
ENV CGO_ENABLED=0
```

You run the Docker build script and try again, and this time it works:

```
$ docker run cookbook/agent agent -h
Usage of agent:
  -version
        show version and exit
```

Discussion

Static executables make life easier for deployment, as long as the OS is recent enough—Linux 2.6.23 or later[3]—and the architecture is the same.

---

2. https://golang.org/cmd/cgo/
3. https://golang.org/dl/

The go build tool tries to create static executables, but in some cases—like our net/http—it will default to using a cgo-based DNS resolver and generate a dynamically linked executable.

If you can, use CGO_ENABLED=0 to force static builds—but you need to know the downside. In our agent case, some DNS resolutions might be wrong. It's up to you to decide if the trade-off is worth it or not.

Recipe 75

Using Build Tags for Conditional Builds

Task

The SRE team says they see some performance degradation in some of the services. It's hard to pinpoint the cause for the performance issues, and you suggest you'll add a profile endpoint to the servers. This can be easily done with the net/http/pprof package, and then you can profile a server in a production environment.

You talk this over with the operations team, and they agree—but with one restriction:

> Some of the servers are customer facing, so for security reasons we'd like the default build to be without a profiling endpoint. Also, we'll build only a couple of servers with the profile endpoint and will tell you which ones these are.

They ask your team to provide a way to run a profiler on a running service so they can pinpoint where the performance degradation is coming from.

Solution

You add the following file next to the web server main code:

building/webprof/prof.go
```
Line 1   //go:build prof
     2
     3   package main
     4
     5   import (
     6       _ "net/http/pprof"
     7   )
```

Then you build the regular web server with go build, and the server with profiling enabled with go build -tags prof.

Discussion

The //go:build prof line tells the go build tool to build the file only if the prof build tag is provided.

Then, in line 6, we do an _ import. When you import net/http/pprof, it registers a /debug/pprof HTTP endpoint with the default HTTP server. Apart from this side effect, you don't use the net/http/pprof module. Since unused modules (and variables) are a compilation error in Go, we prefix the import with _, which tells Go it's OK that we don't use this import.

Build tags were initially designed to support platform-specific code. GOOS and GOARCH are predefined tags. You can use //go:build windows to have a file with Windows-specific code and //go:build linux for Linux-specific code.

File Suffix

 Instead of platform-specific build tags, you can also use file suffixes. For example, a Go file ending with _arm64.go will be built only when GOARCH is arm64, and a Go file ending with _windows.go will be built only on Windows systems.

But apart from platform-specific code, you can use build tags for other conditions, such as our profiling need.

We discussed one example here for building code with or without profiling support. Other examples are loading functionality per client, adding metrics support, and per OS configuration.

Recipe 76

Building Executables for Different Platforms

Task

Your agent is ready for distribution, so you send an email to the marketing team:

Hi,

Finally, the agent is ready for release. Before we can do that, I need to know—what are the combinations of operating system + architecture (for example, Linux on amd64) that we need to support?

The marketing team tell you they need to make some calls, and after a week or so they get back to you with this list:

- Linux with amd64
- Windows with amd64
- OSX with both amd64 and arm64 (the M1/2)

Solution

After some research, you decide to use goreleaser.[4] It does all of what you need and more.

First, you run the following to install goreleaser:

```
$ go install github.com/goreleaser/goreleaser@latest
```

Go Tools

 go install will install tools to the $GOPATH/bin directory. Make sure this directory is in your path.

Here's what I have in my .zshrc:

```
export "PATH=$(go env GOPATH)/bin:${PATH}"
```

After going over the documentation and reading some examples, you write a file called .goreleaser with the following content:

building/multi_agent/.goreleaser.yaml
```yaml
project_name: agent
builds:
  - env:
      - CGO_ENABLED=0
    targets:
      - linux_amd64
      - darwin_arm64
      - darwin_amd64
      - windows_amd64
```

Now you can set the version via a GORELEASER_CURRENT_TAG environment variable and run the following:

```
$ GORELEASER_CURRENT_TAG=v1.2.3 goreleaser build --rm-dist --skip-validate
```

The program runs and emits some output. At the end is a dist directory, and you use the tree command to see what's in it:

```
$ tree
dist
├── agent_darwin_amd64_v1
│   └── agent
├── agent_darwin_arm64
│   └── agent
├── agent_linux_amd64_v1
│   └── agent
├── agent_windows_amd64_v1
│   └── agent.exe
├── artifacts.json
├── config.yaml
└── metadata.json

4 directories, 7 files
```

You also try out a generate executable:

```
$ ./dist/agent_linux_amd64_v1/agent -version
agent version 1.2.3
```

Discussion

By default, goreleaser will use the current git tag for a version. You can override it by setting the GORELEASER_CURRENT_TAG environment variable.

goreleaser can do a lot more: it can run as part of CI/CD and automatically generate artifacts, it can run commands before the build, it can upload artifacts to the GitHub release section, and much more.

gorelease automatically sets the version by injecting it to the executable (see *Injecting Version to Your Executable*). In this task, you already had a version variable, so it worked well for you.

Note that generating executables for different GOOS/GOARCH is not enough; you also need to test your code on these GOOS/GOARCH.

Valid GOOS/GOARCH Combinations

 You can view all the valid GOOS/GOARCH combinations by running go tool dist list.

Recipe 77

Generating Code

Task

Elliot, who's in charge of security, opens the following issue:

> We're starting to get hit by a lot of bots. I'm attaching a list of IPs that are allowed
> to access our services. Please use this list in your code and reject requests not
> coming from an allowed IP. Also, please issue a WARNING security log if a disal-
> lowed IP tries to connect.

These IPs are in a plain-text file with one IP per line, like these, for example:

building/gen/_scripts/allowed_ips.txt
```
127.0.0.1
79.180.16.99
```

Solution

You start by writing a Go script that will convert the text file into a Go file
containing a map with all the allowed IPs.

First, you declare the generated Go file header:

building/gen/_scripts/gen_ips.go
```go
var header = `
package main

// IPAllowed returns true if connections from ip are allowed
func IPAllowed(ip string) bool {
    return allowedIPs[ip]
}

var allowedIPs = map[string]bool{`
```

Then, in main you open the input and output files:

building/gen/_scripts/gen_ips.go
```go
in, err := os.Open(os.Args[1])
if err != nil {
    log.Fatalf("error: %s", err)
}
defer in.Close()
```

```
out, err := os.Create(os.Args[2])
if err != nil {
    log.Fatalf("error: %s", err)
}
defer out.Close()
```

And then you generate the Go code:

```
fmt.Fprintln(out, header)

s := bufio.NewScanner(in)
for s.Scan() {
    fmt.Fprintf(out, "%q: true,\n", s.Text())
}

if err := s.Err(); err != nil {
    log.Fatalf("error: %s", err)
}

fmt.Fprintln(out, "}")
```

To automate generating the code, you add a go generate directive to one of the application files:

```
//go:generate go run _scripts/gen_ips.go _scripts/allowed_ips.txt ips.go
//go:generate go fmt ips.go
```

You create a function to extract the IP from a *http.Request:

```
func requestIP(r *http.Request) string {
    fields := strings.Split(r.RemoteAddr, ":")
    if len(fields) != 2 {
        return ""
    }

    return fields[0]
}
```

Finally, you can use the code in your handlers:

```
if ip := requestIP(r); !IPAllowed(ip) {
    log.Printf("WARNING: (sec) access from disallowed IP: %s", ip)
    http.Error(w, "Unknown IP", http.StatusUnauthorized)
    return
}
```

Discussion

Code that generates code is an old and established technique. In his book, *The Art of Unix Programming*, Eric Raymond describes it as the Rule of Generation: avoid hand-hacking; write programs to write programs when you can.

Generating code has several advantages:

No serialization
> The data is in Go, and you don't need to unmarshal it. As you saw in *Serializing Data*, serialization is tricky to get right.

Single File
> You don't need to ship extra files other than the executable. Shipping a single executable is much easier than shipping two or more files.

Catching Errors Faster
> If you don't generate a valid Go file, the compilation will fail. If you use embed, for example, and then parse the file at runtime, the error will happen later in the development chain, which usually means more effort to fix.

The code for generation is in the _script directory. The go build command ignores files and directories that start with _. Another option to have gen_ips.go ignored by the go build command is to add a //go:build ignore directive to the top of gen_ips.go.

The downside of the code-generation approach is that building the code is now two steps: go generate and then go build. Developers are bound to forget a step, so use some kind of automation for the build (for example, a Makefile).

On the other hand, if you don't keep the generated files in source control, users who get a fresh copy of the code won't be able to build it without running go generate.

A debate is ongoing about keeping generated files in source control. If you keep the generated files in source control, then building the code gets back to being a simple go build, but you're raising the chance that allowed_ips.txt will be updated and the generated code won't.

Which approach to take? That's up to you—weigh the pros and cons and decide. Personally, I do keep the generated code in source control.

Final Thoughts

Most of the time your builds will be simple: run go build and you have an executable ready to be deployed. The go build system has many features that will cover most of your needs. We've seen how you can add data into your application, inject values into the generated executable, and force static builds. I'm sure that you'll find more ways to make go build work to your advantage.

Delivering a simple executable has enormous value. Delivering more than one file to production is much more complex; you need to know where to place these files, and your application needs to know where to find them. I recommend sticking to a single file deployment as much as you can.

I tried to cover go build capabilities that I think you'll find useful. In case you didn't find a solution to your needs here, head over to the go build documentation, where you'll see many more options documented.

Next, we'll see what happens after you've built your program—how you can ship it.

## CHAPTER 15

Shipping Your Code

The only place where your code has business value is production. You can add features, fix bugs, and optimize for performance as much as you want. But as long as your code is not running in production, it has close to zero business value.

Production is where your code goes out of the cozy development or QA environment into the harsh world of production. In production, anything that can go wrong eventually will. You need to prepare your code for this harsh environment. You also need to know if something goes wrong and *why* ideally before your clients notice.

You also need to decouple your code from environment changes. If your server needs to listen on a different port, there's no reason you should change the code to accommodate this change.

In this chapter, we'll talk about all these points and more—from managing dependencies to logging and configuration.

Recipe 78

Configuring Your Application

Task

After several all-nighters, your server is finally ready to be shipped to production. You start the morning by going through your inbox and come across an email titled "Production Readiness Checklist" from the operations team. The email describes what a server must support to be production ready. Going down the list, you see that most of it is already implemented. However, one section is still missing—configuration.

The email says:

> The application should support configuration via environment variables with an application prefix or command line. At least two options should be supported: address to listen on and logging level.
>
> Examples:
>
> $ APP_ADDR=localhost:9999 ./app
> $ ./app --web-addr=localhost:9999

Solution

You decide to start by implementing support for address only and, once done, implementing support for log level. After a survey of configuration packages, you decide to use github.com/ardanlabs/conf. You start by importing the package:

ship/config/app.go
```
"github.com/ardanlabs/conf/v3"
```

Since the package is in version 3, you add the /v3 suffix in the import path.

Next, you define the configuration structure, which is an anonymous struct:

ship/config/app.go
```
Line 1  var cfg struct {
     2      Web struct {
     3          Addr string `conf:"default::8080,env:ADDR"`
     4      }
     5  }
```

In 3, you use field tags to define the name of the environment variable and the default value.

Then you use the conf package to parse the configuration:

ship/config/app.go
```
help, err := conf.Parse("APP", &cfg)
if err != nil {
    if errors.Is(err, conf.ErrHelpWanted) {
        fmt.Println(help)
        os.Exit(0)
    }
    log.Fatalf("error: bad config - %s", err)
}
```

After configuration is parsed, you still need to validate it:

```
ship/config/app.go
if err := validateAddr(cfg.Web.Addr); err != nil {
    log.Fatalf("error: invalid config - %s", err)
}
```

Here's how you validate the address:

```
ship/config/app.go
func validateAddr(addr string) error {
    i := strings.Index(addr, ":")
    if i == -1 {
        return fmt.Errorf("%q: missing : in address", addr)
    }

    port, err := strconv.Atoi(addr[i+1:])
    if err != nil {
        return fmt.Errorf("%q: invalid port - %w", addr, err)
    }

    const maxPort = 65_535
    if port < 0 || port > maxPort {
        return fmt.Errorf("%q: invalid port number", addr)
    }

    return nil
}
```

Now you can test your code:

```
$ go run app.go
{Web:{Addr::8080}}
$ APP_ADDR=:9999 go run app.go
{Web:{Addr::9999}}
$ APP_ADDR=:9999999 go run app.go
2022/11/10 19:13:53 error: invalid config - ":9999999": invalid port number
$ go run app.go --web-addr=:9999
{Web:{Addr::9999}}
```

Looks good.

Discussion

Application configuration has a traditional hierarchy:

1. Defaults
2. Configuration file
3. Environment variables
4. Command-line options

You don't need to support all of these options—make sure to be in sync with the operations team and see what you need. Go has several configuration packages, such as viper and its relative cobra. You can even stay in the standard library, using flag to parse the command line and os.Getenv to read the environment. Make sure to evaluate your solution and see that it fits your needs.

Configuration is important; it separates policy from mechanism. But try not to have too many configuration options. Even if each configuration option is yes/no, for ten options you have $2^{10} = 1024$ possibilities to test. It's hard to say no to yet another configuration option—but do try. Go is a good example of providing great code without too many options.

Last, but most important in my eyes: validate your configuration before you start your application. If you read incident reports companies are publishing, you'll see that many of these incidents were caused by bad configuration.

Recipe 79

Patching Dependencies

Task

You're working in an exciting new space company.

You're in charge of the simulation software. To speed up development, you decide to use an existing third-party package: github.com/353solutions/geo.

Progress is great, until you hit a bug in the Euclidean distance function. You head over to the package site and open a bug:

> Title: Overflow in Euclidean
> Hi. Thanks for a great package. I've found an overflow bug in the Euclidean function. For example, Euclidean(0, 0, 95e200, 168e200) returns +Inf, but it should return 1.9300000000000002e+202

The developer answers:

> Hi. Thanks! Sorry for the bug. I'm flying out tomorrow to hike the Appalachian Trail. I'll fix the bug when I'm back in about three months.

Ouch!

Solution

You start by writing a test to reproduce the bug:

ship/simulator/sim_test.go
```
func TestEuclideanBug(t *testing.T) {
    d := geo.Euclidean(0, 0, 95e200, 168e200)
    if math.IsInf(d, 1) {
        t.Fatal(d)
    }
}
```

And when you run it, you see it fails:

```
$ go test -v
=== RUN   TestEuclideanBug
    sim_test.go:14: +Inf
--- FAIL: TestEuclideanBug (0.00s)
FAIL
exit status 1
FAIL    git.spacey.com/sim      0.002s
```

Then you copy the geo project to the _patch directory and add a replace line in the project's go.mod file:

ship/simulator/go.mod
```
module git.spacey.com/sim

go 1.19

require github.com/353solutions/geo v1.2.3

replace github.com/353solutions/geo => ./_patch/geo
```

Now you can fix the bug in your local copy:

ship/simulator/_patch/geo/geo.go
```
func Euclidean(x1, y1, x2, y2 float64) float64 {
    dx := x1 - x2
    dy := y1 - y2

    // Hypot won't under/overflow
    return math.Hypot(dx, dy)
}
```

Finally, you run your test again:

```
$ go test -v
=== RUN   TestEuclideanBug
--- PASS: TestEuclideanBug (0.00s)
PASS
ok      git.spacey.com/sim      0.002s
```

Discussion

Most open source projects are maintained by one or two developers, and it's not their primary job. At one point or another, you'll have to fork a project and keep your own copy with bug fixes or new features.

You have several options:

Fork

> You can copy the project to another git repository (say git.spacey.com/geo). The downside of this approach is that you will need to change all the import paths inside your project.

Vendor

> A second approach is to vendor your dependencies. When you run go mod vendor, Go will create a vendor directory with all your dependencies. When you build/test/run your code, Go will use the dependencies from the vendor directory. The downside of this approach is that the vendor directory might be very big. Also, every time you update your dependencies, it shows as a very big diff.

Replace

> This is the approach you took; it minimizes the amount of external code in your repository.

Which approach is best? That's up to you and your team. You should consider the pros and cons of each approach and make an informed decision. Personally, I tend to use replace for a problem I know will be fixed in the short term and vendoring for the long run.

---

go.mod

Go modules have many more features than "just" specifying requirements. You can direct to an internal module host by setting the GOPROXY environment variable, you can explicitly disallow specific versions using an exclude directive, and more.

Head over to https://go.dev/ref/mod and read the documentation.

Recipe 80

Packaging Applications in Docker

Task

Finally, the database API service is tested and ready to go!

You chat with Lily from the operations team about how they are going to deploy it. Lily writes:

> We use Docker to ship all of the services now. We think it's better that you write the initial Dockerfile, and then we'll tweak it to our needs. Please use debian:bookworm-slim as base image.

You brush up on Docker documentation and start to code.

Solution

You add a Dockerfile to the root of your project with a couple of sections. The first is the build section, which uses the golang:1.20-bookworm as base image:

ship/dbq/Dockerfile
```
FROM golang:1.20-bookworm AS build
WORKDIR /build
COPY go.mod go.sum ./
RUN go mod download
COPY . .
ENV CGO_ENABLED=0
RUN go build -o ./dbq
```

The second (and final) stage uses debian:bookworm-slim as base image for deployment:

ship/dbq/Dockerfile
```
FROM debian:bookworm-slim
COPY --from=build /build/dbq /usr/local/bin

# Don't run as root user
RUN groupadd -r app && useradd --no-log-init -r -g app app
USER app

CMD dbq
```

Discussion

Once you build a Go executable, you don't need the Go SDK anymore (unlike, say, Java, which requires a JVM installed to run).

Let's have a look at the Docker image sizes:

```
$ docker images | grep bookworm
golang          1.20-bookworm    99f8cec02f0a    11 hours ago    845MB
debian          bookworm-slim    7016e0cd8b19    5 days ago      74.8MB
```

The bookwork-slim debian image is about eleven times smaller than the golang image we used to build. Smaller images will save you money, both on storage and the bandwidth to move them around. By using a multistage docker build, you greatly reduce the size of the final image.

Docker caches every build step. You use this to your advantage by first copying go.mod and go.sum and running go mod download. After this step, you copy over the source files and build them. Since the source files change more frequently than the dependencies specific in go.mod, the go mod download step will be cached most of the time.

The line ENV CGO_ENABLED=0 forces Go to build a static executable that does not rely on external shared libraries. Docker helps with the problem of shared libraries on Linux, but I prefer to be extra careful and use static binaries—there might be some difference in the shared libraries installed on the build image versus the deployment images.

Building Docker

 Building Docker images is an art in itself—there are many considerations that you'll want to think about when using it. For example, it's not a good idea to run the application as the root user.

You'll want to create a user for the application on the final docker and have it run the application. See https://docs.docker.com/develop/develop-images/dockerfile_best-practices/ for more details.

Recipe 81

Catching Signals for Graceful Shutdown

Task

Jack from the operations team opens a chat:

> Hi. We're using kill to terminate services. We noticed that when we terminate your server, it drops connections immediately. Can you please make sure the server is doing a graceful shutdown when it's being terminated?

You start working.

Signals

Signals are standard notifications that are sent to running processes. Signals have been around since the 1970s and are often used to notify running servers they need to shut down or reload configuration. For example, every time you hit CTRL-C, a signal called SIGINT is sent to the current process.

You can read more about signals at https://man7.org/linux/man-pages/man7/signal.7.html.

Solution

You start by creating your own HTTP server and not using the default one:

```
ship/signal/signal.go
mux := http.NewServeMux()
mux.HandleFunc("/health", healthHandler)

addr := ":8080"
srv := &http.Server{
    Addr:    addr,
    Handler: mux,
}
```

Then you run the server in a goroutine:

```
ship/signal/signal.go
go func() {
    log.Printf("server starting on %s", addr)
    err := srv.ListenAndServe()
```

```
    if err != nil && err != http.ErrServerClosed {
        log.Printf("error: listen - %s", err)
        os.Exit(1)
    }
}()
```

Now you can start taking care of signals. First you tell the Go runtime to direct signals to a buffered channel:

ship/signal/signal.go

```
Line 1  ch := make(chan os.Signal, 1)
     2  signal.Notify(ch, unix.SIGTERM, unix.SIGINT)
```

Finally, you receive from the channel and initiate a graceful shutdown:

ship/signal/signal.go

```
<-ch
log.Printf("shutting down")
ctx, cancel := context.WithTimeout(context.Background(), time.Second)
defer cancel()
if err := srv.Shutdown(ctx); err != nil {
    log.Printf("error: shutdown - %s", err)
}
```

Discussion

The signal package documentation[1] says:

> By default, a synchronous signal is converted into a runtime panic. A SIGHUP, SIGINT, or SIGTERM signal causes the program to exit. A SIGQUIT, SIGILL, SIGTRAP, SIGABRT, SIGSTKFLT, SIGEMT, or SIGSYS signal causes the program to exit with a stack dump. A SIGTSTP, SIGTTIN, or SIGTTOU signal gets the system default behavior (these signals are used by the shell for job control). The SIGPROF signal is handled directly by the Go runtime to implement runtime.CPUProfile. Other signals will be caught, but no action will be taken.

Those are a lot of signals! I won't go into detail about what each signal means—you can run man 7 signal in your Unix shell to learn more about all these kinds of signals.

Sending and catching signals is an old Unix tradition. The two most common signals to terminate a process are SIGINT, which is caused when a user presses CONTROL-C, and SIGTERM, which is the default signal the kill command sends. These are the signals we catch on line 2. Note that ch on line 1 must be buffered.

The built-in HTTP server supports graceful shutdown. Do read the documentation[2] about how this shutdown behaves. You can also use signal handling

---

1.   https://pkg.go.dev/os/signal
2.   https://pkg.go.dev/net/http#Server.Shutdown

to clean other resources upon exit—maybe a process you spawn or some temporary files.

Design Consideration

I chose to run the server in a goroutine and handle signals in main. I've seen the other approach, where the server runs in main and the signal handling is done in a goroutine. I don't have a strong preference either way, but exiting the program from main (versus a goroutine) feels more natural to me.

Recipe 82

Writing Logs

Task

Ruby from the SRE team opens an issue:

> We're seeing some performance issues with the latest version's server. This is the version that added token-based authentication. Can you please check?

After doing some git-bisect, you see that Ruby is right (as usual) and start to look for the issue.

Solution

You take a look at the login code:

ship/log/log.go
```
Line 1  // Login authenticates user from token and returns user id
   -    func (s *Server) login(token string) (int, error) {
   -        uid, err := auth.Authenticate(token) // API call to auth service
   -        if err != nil {
   5            return 0, err
   -        }
   -
   -        s.logger.Info("logged in",
   -            zap.Any("user", users.Load(uid)),
   10       )
   -
   -        return uid, nil
   -    }
```

Nothing seems suspicious, so you fire up the profiler and load test the server. The profiler reports that line 8 is taking most of the time.

Weird! The logging level set in your application is Error, and you don't see these logs generated. Why does this code take so much time?

The answer is that you do a call to users.Load regardless of the configured log level.

Looking at the documentation, you find out you can check if a level is enabled or not before starting the work.

You change login to the following:

```
ship/log_check/log.go
// Login authenticates user from token and returns user id
func (s *Server) login(token string) (int, error) {
    uid, err := auth.Authenticate(token) // API call to auth service
    if err != nil {
        return 0, err
    }

    if info := s.logger.Check(zap.InfoLevel, "logged in"); info != nil {
        info.Write(
            zap.Any("user", users.Load(uid)),
        )
    }

    return uid, nil
}
```

If zap.InfoLevel is enabled, info will be an entry with the message set to "logged in"; otherwise, it will be nil. Now the call to users.Load will happen only if zap.InfoLevel is enabled.

Note we use info.Write (and not info.Info) since the info already has the level set.

You run the profiler again and see that login now takes very little time to run.

Discussion

Logging
by: Bill Kennedy

If logging doesn't help you during development, it's for sure not going to help you in production.

Logging is important; it's your eyes to production, and you should emit as much context as possible to the logs. However, logging can slow your application, sometimes by a lot.

Go evaluates parameters to a function before calling it. This is the expected behavior, but in some cases, it can have performance implications.

Get to know your logging system; most of them provide similar functionality to check if a level is enabled.

Recipe 83

Using Metrics as Eyes to Production

Task

You're working on a server that does reverse geocoding. The server API gets a latitude and longitude and returns an address.

Before you deploy the server to production, you meet with the operations team. They tell you that to monitor your service, the server needs to publish some metrics. These metrics should be the number of calls to the server, the number of calls that were successful, and the number of calls that failed.

You agree that it's a great idea and start working on it.

Solution

You decide to use the built-in expvar package. It publishes metrics in a JSON format, and the operations team said they can collect these metrics.

Knowing the number of calls is easy, but to know if a handler failed, you need to detect the HTTP error code it emitted. You start by writing your own http.ResponseWriter that keeps the emitted HTTP code:

```
ship/metrics/httpd.go
Line 1  type statusWriter struct {
     2      http.ResponseWriter
     3      statusCode          int
     4  }
     5
     6  func (s *statusWriter) WriteHeader(status int) {
     7      s.statusCode = status
     8      s.ResponseWriter.WriteHeader(status)
     9  }
```

Your statusWriter embeds another http.ResponseWriter (see line 2). Then it implements only the WriteHeader method, which will store the status code and call WriteHeader of the embedded http.ResponseWriter.

Once you have statusWriter in place, you can write the addMetrics middleware:

ship/metrics/httpd.go
```go
func addMetrics(name string, h http.Handler) http.Handler {
    calls := expvar.NewInt(fmt.Sprintf("%s.calls", name))
    errors := expvar.NewInt(fmt.Sprintf("%s.errors", name))
    oks := expvar.NewInt(fmt.Sprintf("%s.oks", name))

    fn := func(w http.ResponseWriter, r *http.Request) {
        calls.Add(1)

        sw := statusWriter{w, http.StatusOK}
        h.ServeHTTP(&sw, r)

        if sw.statusCode >= http.StatusBadRequest {
            errors.Add(1)
        } else {
            oks.Add(1)
        }
    }

    return http.HandlerFunc(fn)
}
```

First, you create three metrics, for number of calls, errors, and ... not errors. Inside the inner fn function you first increment the calls metrics, then replace the original http.ResponseWriter with your statusWriter. Once the original handler is done, you check the status code it emitted and update either errors or oks.

Finally, when you create the routing, you wrap the original lookupHandler with addMetrics:

ship/metrics/httpd.go
```go
h := addMetrics("lookup", http.HandlerFunc(lookupHandler))
http.Handle("/lookup", h)
```

For completeness, here's the (redacted) implementation of lookupHandler:

ship/metrics/httpd.go
```go
func lookupHandler(w http.ResponseWriter, r *http.Request) {
    lat, err := strconv.ParseFloat(r.URL.Query().Get("lat"), 64)
    if err != nil || lat < -90 || lat > 90 {
        http.Error(w, "bad lat", http.StatusBadRequest)
        return
    }
```

```go
    lng, err := strconv.ParseFloat(r.URL.Query().Get("lng"), 64)
    if err != nil || lng < -180 || lng > 180 {
        http.Error(w, "bad lng", http.StatusBadRequest)
        return
    }
    // Lookup code redacted
    fmt.Fprintln(w, "Earth")
}
```

Now you can try it out. You run your server and make a couple of calls. Finally, you hit /debug/vars and see your metrics:

ship/metrics/test.sh
```bash
#!/bin/bash

# OK call
curl -i 'http://localhost:8080/lookup?lat=1&lng=2'

# Error (invalid latitude)
curl -i 'http://localhost:8080/lookup?lat=100&lng=2'

# Check metrics
curl 'http://localhost:8080/debug/vars'
```

Somewhere inside the output of the last command you see this:

```
"lookup.calls": 2,
"lookup.errors": 1,
"lookup.oks": 1,
```

Discussion

Metrics can be either pulled by a monitoring system (such as Prometheus[3]) or pushed to it. The expvar package is designed to be pulled on; it publishes the metrics in JSON format under /debug/vars. If you use a different router, you might need to install the expvar endpoint manually using expvar.Handler.

On HTTP servers, the best way to to add metrics is via middleware. See *Writing Middleware to Monitor Performance* for more details.

Metrics are your eyes to production. You should design them and monitor them. It's also good to have an alerting system that will wake someone (usually at 4 a.m.) if a metric goes awry.

---

3. https://prometheus.io/

Recipe 84

Debugging Running Services

Task

You are in charge of a messaging system. The data engineering team opens an issue for you:

> For some reason, we see several empty messages in the database. We *think* it comes from your code and not our process. Can you please check.

You think it's probably not from your code, since you *do* validate input messages before you continue. But you know the data engineering team are very professional, so you can't discard their claim.

Looking at the code, you don't see anything suspicious:

ship/messaging/httpd.go

```go
// Message is a channel message.
type Message struct {
    From    string `json:"from"`
    Channel string `json:"channel"`
    Body    string `json:"body"`

    ID string `json:"-"`
}

func addHandler(w http.ResponseWriter, r *http.Request) {
    var m Message
    if err := json.NewDecoder(r.Body).Decode(&m); err != nil {
        log.Printf("error: bad JSON - %s", err)
        http.Error(w, "bad JSON", http.StatusBadRequest)
    }

    m.ID = uuid.NewString()
    // Adding code redacted

    resp := map[string]any{
        "id":   m.ID,
        "time": time.Now().UTC(),
    }
    data, err := json.Marshal(resp)
    if err != nil {
        log.Printf("error: can't marshal JSON - %s", err)
        http.Error(w, "can't marshal JSON", http.StatusInternalServerError)
        return
    }
```

```
    w.Header().Set("Content-Type", "application/json")
    if _, err := w.Write(data); err != nil {
        log.Printf("error: can't send - %s", err)
    }
}
```

It's complicated to generate a full copy of the production environment on your machine for debugging. You ask the operations team to keep the problematic service alive and divert traffic to the older version. This way, you have a running service you can debug.

Solution

You SSH to the machine where the service is running. First, you find the service process ID:

```
$ ps aux | grep messag
miki        608230  0.0  0.0 1085896 7120 pts/0    Sl+  19:12    0:00 ./messaging
miki        608548  0.0  0.0    6572 2376 pts/1    S+   19:12    0:00 grep messag
```

The first match is the service process, and the second is the grep command you just ran.

Once you have the server process ID, 608230, you run the following:

```
$ sudo dlv attach 608230
Type 'help' for list of commands.
(dlv)
```

You're now in the dlv debugger textual user interface (TUI). Now you can set a breakpoint:

```
(dlv) b main.addHandler
Breakpoint 1 set at 0x64a04f for main.addHandler() ./httpd.go:21
(dlv) c
```

Now you have a breakpoint at the handler. The c command resumes the process.

Next, from another shell, you hit the API:

```
$ curl -d'BAD JSON' http://localhost:8080/messages
```

The curl call gets stuck, but when you switch to dlv you now see this:

```
> main.addHandler() ./httpd.go:21 (hits goroutine(34):1 total:1) (PC: 0x64a04f)
Warning: debugging optimized function
Warning: listing may not match stale executable
    16:         Channel string `json:"channel"`
    17:         Body    string `json:"body"`
    18:
    19:         ID string `json:"-"`
    20: }
=>  21:
    22: func addHandler(w http.ResponseWriter, r *http.Request) {
    23:         var m Message
    24:         if err := json.NewDecoder(r.Body).Decode(&m); err != nil {
    25:                 log.Printf("ERROR: bad JSON - %s", err)
    26:                 http.Error(w, "bad JSON", http.StatusBadRequest)
```

You hit the breakpoint, and now you can debug. You move the code by running n (for next). After hitting n a few times, you see the problem. You forgot to add retrun after http.Error

Now you hit q for "quit":

```
(dlv) q
Would you like to kill the process? [Y/n]
```

You hit Y since you don't need the service anymore. You logout from the remote machine and tell the operations team they can tear it down.

Finally, you fix the bug by writing a failing test; then you fix the problem by adding a return statement.

Discussion

Delve[4] is *the* Go debugger; the command to run it is dlv. It's usually easier to use dlv from your IDE, but in some cases this isn't possible. The Delve debugger also has a textual interface that can be used in an SSH session on remote machines. The textual user interface might take some time to learn, but the help command will show you most of what you need.

Attaching to a running process requires elevated privileges, which is why you used sudo before the dlv attach command.

---

4.   https://github.com/go-delve/delve

Installing Delve

You'll need to install Delve before you can start using it. You can install it by running go install github.com/go-delve/delve/cmd/dlv@latest. The dlv command will be installed to $GOPATH/bin, so make sure this directory is in your $PATH. If you don't know the value of $GOPATH, run go env GOPATH.

Final Thoughts

Production is a harsh place. Disks get full, connections time out, and even plain bugs can cause your application to malfunction—not to mention the users, who do all kinds of funny stuff. In this chapter, we discussed ways that will help your code survive in production. Testing, handling dependencies, Docker packaging, and other techniques make it easy for your code to be deployed.

Once you've deployed software once or twice, you know errors *will* happen. Metrics are your eyes to production, and once you detect a problem by using them, you can use the logs to find out *why* there's an issue.

As you gain more experience in shipping code, you'll develop more practices that will make those 4 a.m. pager-duty calls less frequent.

Index

Thank you!

We hope you enjoyed this book and that you're already thinking about what you want to learn next. To help make that decision easier, we're offering you this gift.

Head on over to https://pragprog.com right now, and use the coupon code BUYANOTHER2024 to save 30% on your next ebook. Offer is void where prohibited or restricted. This offer does not apply to any edition of *The Pragmatic Programmer* ebook.

And if you'd like to share your own expertise with the world, why not propose a writing idea to us? After all, many of our best authors started off as our readers, just like you. With up to a 50% royalty, world-class editorial services, and a name you trust, there's nothing to lose. Visit https://pragprog.com/become-an-author/ today to learn more and to get started.

Thank you for your continued support. We hope to hear from you again soon!

The Pragmatic Bookshelf

Go Brain Teasers

This book contains 25 short programs that will challenge your understanding of Go. Like any big project, the Go developers had to make some design decisions that at times seem surprising. This book uses those quirks as a teaching opportunity. By understanding the gaps in your knowledge, you'll become better at what you do. Some of the teasers are from the author's experience shipping bugs to production, and some from others doing the same. Teasers and puzzles are fun, and learning how to solve them can teach you to avoid programming mistakes and maybe even impress your colleagues and future employers.

Miki Tebeka
(110 pages) ISBN: 9781680508994. $18.95
https://pragprog.com/book/d-gobrain

Python Brain Teasers

We geeks love puzzles and solving them. The Python programming language is a simple one, but like all other languages it has quirks. This book uses those quirks as teaching opportunities via 30 simple Python programs that challenge your understanding of Python. The teasers will help you avoid mistakes, see gaps in your knowledge, and become better at what you do. Use these teasers to impress your co-workers or just to pass the time in those boring meetings. Teasers are fun!

Miki Tebeka
(116 pages) ISBN: 9781680509007. $18.95
https://pragprog.com/book/d-pybrain

Pandas Brain Teasers

This book contains 25 short programs that will challenge your understanding of Pandas. Like any big project, the Pandas developers had to make some design decisions that at times seem surprising. This book uses those quirks as a teaching opportunity. By understanding the gaps in your knowledge, you'll become better at what you do. Some of the teasers are from the author's experience shipping bugs to production, and some from others doing the same. Teasers and puzzles are fun, and learning how to solve them can teach you to avoid programming mistakes and maybe even impress your colleagues and future employers.

Miki Tebeka
(110 pages) ISBN: 9781680509014. $18.95
https://pragprog.com/book/d-pandas

Powerful Command-Line Applications in Go

Write your own fast, reliable, and cross platform command-line tools with the Go programming language. Go might be the fastest—and perhaps the most fun—way to automate tasks, analyze data, parse logs, talk to network services, or address other systems requirements. Create all kinds of command-line tools that work with files, connect to services, and manage external processes, all while using tests and benchmarks to ensure your programs are fast and correct.

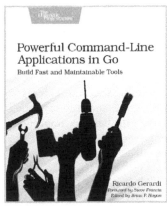

Ricardo Gerardi
(508 pages) ISBN: 9781680506969. $45.95
https://pragprog.com/book/rggo

JavaScript Brain Teasers

If you've ever felt the exhilaration of cracking a thorny problem or the joy of witnessing elegant code that challenges your mind, then this book is tailor-made for you. Prepare yourself to dive into a diverse array of mind-bending JavaScript brain teasers. Each puzzle is more than just a code exercise; it's a gateway to unlocking new insights and honing your abilities. As you work through the challenges, you'll learn to think pragmatically, optimize your code for efficiency, and avoid hidden pitfalls that can catch you off guard. What's more—the puzzle format will help you remember what you've learned!

Faraz K. Kelhini
(128 pages) ISBN: 9798888650523. $32.95
https://pragprog.com/book/fkjsbrain

C Brain Teasers

You thought you knew C, but can you solve 25 puzzles in this popular programming language? Noted C programmer and author Dan Gookin provides a series of pointed questions, puzzles, and problems to keep your C programming skills sharp. Each one will provide insight into various aspects of handling strings, numeric operations, and other activities, giving you techniques to take the best advantage of all C has to offer. Challenge yourself, and get to know some powerful tricks and details for writing better, faster, more accurate C code.

Dan Gookin
(118 pages) ISBN: 9798888650486. $32.95
https://pragprog.com/book/cbrain

Agile Retrospectives, Second Edition

In an uncertain and complex world, learning is more important than ever before. In fact, it can be a competitive advantage. Teams and organizations that learn rapidly deliver greater customer value faster and more reliably. Furthermore, those teams are more engaged, more productive, and more satisfied. The most effective way to enable teams to learn is by holding regular retrospectives. Unfortunately, many teams only get shallow results from their retrospectives. This book is filled with practical advice, techniques, and real-life examples that will take retrospectives to the next level—whether your team is co-located, hybrid, or remote. This book will help team leads, scrum masters, and coaches engage their teams to learn, improve, and deliver greater results.

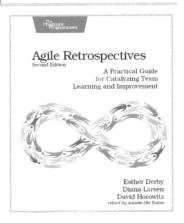

Esther Derby, Diana Larsen, David Horowitz
(298 pages) ISBN: 9798888650370. $53.95
https://pragprog.com/book/dlret2

Charged Bodies

At the heart of Silicon Valley's meteoric rise is a story etched in the lives of those who shaped it and those who were forever transformed by it. Author Tom Mahon provides an insider's perspective on the birth of the semiconductor industry, which sparked the region's transformation from sleepy farmland to the heart and soul of the high-tech revolution. Through twenty-five extended, in-person interviews you'll meet a diverse cast of characters whose goal was to create technology and tools in service to humanity. In the Afterword to this edition, the author questions whether they accomplished their objectives and urges readers to rise up and rethink technology.

Thomas Mahon
(330 pages) ISBN: 9798888650592. $27.95
https://pragprog.com/book/tmbodies

The Pragmatic Bookshelf

The Pragmatic Bookshelf features books written by professional developers for professional developers. The titles continue the well-known Pragmatic Programmer style and continue to garner awards and rave reviews. As development gets more and more difficult, the Pragmatic Programmers will be there with more titles and products to help you stay on top of your game.

Visit Us Online

This Book's Home Page
https://pragprog.com/book/mtgo
Source code from this book, errata, and other resources. Come give us feedback, too!

Keep Up-to-Date
https://pragprog.com
Join our announcement mailing list (low volume) or follow us on Twitter @pragprog for new titles, sales, coupons, hot tips, and more.

New and Noteworthy
https://pragprog.com/news
Check out the latest Pragmatic developments, new titles, and other offerings.

Save on the ebook

Save on the ebook versions of this title. Owning the paper version of this book entitles you to purchase the electronic versions at a terrific discount.

PDFs are great for carrying around on your laptop—they are hyperlinked, have color, and are fully searchable. Most titles are also available for the iPhone and iPod touch, Amazon Kindle, and other popular e-book readers.

Send a copy of your receipt to support@pragprog.com and we'll provide you with a discount coupon.

Contact Us

Online Orders:	*https://pragprog.com/catalog*
Customer Service:	*support@pragprog.com*
International Rights:	*translations@pragprog.com*
Academic Use:	*academic@pragprog.com*
Write for Us:	*http://write-for-us.pragprog.com*

Milton Keynes UK
Ingram Content Group UK Ltd.
UKHW050610310524
443454UK00001B/5